DATE DUE

THE HARVARD BUSINESS REVIEW PAPERBACK SERIES

The series is designed to bring today's managers and professionals the fundamental information they need to stay competitive in a fast-moving world. From the preeminent thinkers whose work has defined an entire field to the rising stars who will redefine the way we think about business, here are the leading minds and landmark ideas that have established the *Harvard Business Review* as required reading for ambitious businesspeople in organizations around the globe.

Other books in the series:

Harvard Business Review

ON

STRATEGIC ALLIANCES

A HARVARD BUSINESS REVIEW PAPERBACK

The *Harvard Business Review* articles in this collection are available as
individual reprints. Discounts apply to quantity purchases. For information and ordering, please contact Customer Service, Harvard Business
School Publishing, Boston, MA 02163. Telephone: (617) 783-7500 or
(800) 988-0886, 8 A.M. to 6 P.M. Eastern Time, Monday through Friday.
Fax: (617) 783-7555, 24 hours a day. E-mail: custserv@hbsp.harvard.edu

Library of Congress Cataloging-in-Publication Data
Harvard business review on strategic alliances.
        p.   cm. — (A Harvard business review paperback)
    Includes index.
    ISBN 1-59139-133-4 (alk. paper)
    1. Strategic alliances (Business).   I. Harvard Business School Press.
II. Harvard business review.   III. Harvard business review paperback
series.
HD69.S8 H377   2002
338.8´7—dc21   2002012683
                                                                      CIP

*The paper used in this publication meets the requirements of the Ameri-
can National Standard for Permanence of Paper for Publications and
Documents in Libraries and Archives Z39.48-1992.*

Contents

Collaborate with Your Competitors—and Win

GARY HAMEL, YVES L. DOZ, AND
C.K. PRAHALAD

Executive Summary

COLLABORATION BETWEEN COMPETITORS is in fashion. General Motors and Toyota assemble automobiles, Siemens and Philips develop semiconductors, and Canon supplies photocopiers to Kodak. But the rise of competitive collaboration has triggered unease about its long-term effects. In particular, alliances between Asian companies and their Western rivals seem to work against the Western partner. Cooperation leads to competitive surrender.

Many Western companies do give away more than they gain—but that's because they enter partnerships without knowing what it takes to win. Companies that benefit most from competitive collaboration adhere to a set of simple but powerful principles.

Collaboration is competition in a different form. Successful companies never forget that their partners may be

1

out to disarm them. They understand how their partners' objectives compare with their own.

Harmony is not the most important measure of success. Indeed, occasional conflict may be the best evidence of mutually beneficial collaboration. Few alliances remain win-win undertakings forever.

Partners must defend against competitive compromise. What information gets traded is determined daily, often by junior engineers and operating managers. Successful companies inform employees at all levels about what skills and technologies are off-limits to the partner.

Learning from partners is paramount. Successful companies view each alliance as a window on their partners' broad capabilities. They use the alliance to build skills in areas outside the formal agreement and to diffuse acquired knowledge throughout their organizations.

COLLABORATION BETWEEN COMPETITORS is in fashion. General Motors and Toyota assemble automobiles, Siemens and Philips develop semiconductors, Canon supplies photocopiers to Kodak, France's Thomson and Japan's JVC manufacture videocassette recorders. But the spread of what we call "competitive collaboration"—joint ventures, out-sourcing agreements, product licensings, cooperative research—has triggered unease about the long-term consequences. A strategic alliance can strengthen both companies against outsiders even as it weakens one partner vis-à-vis the other. In particular, alliances between Asian companies and Western rivals seem to work against the Western partner. Cooperation becomes a low-cost route for new competitors to gain technology and market access.[1]

Yet the case for collaboration is stronger than ever. It takes so much money to develop new products and to penetrate new markets that few companies can go it alone in every situation. ICL, the British computer company, could not have developed its current generation of mainframes without Fujitsu. Motorola needs Toshiba's distribution capacity to break into the Japanese semiconductor market. Time is another critical factor. Alliances can provide short-cuts for Western companies racing to improve their production efficiency and quality control.

We have spent more than five years studying the inner workings of 15 strategic alliances and monitoring scores of others. Our research (see "About Our Research" at the end of this article) involves cooperative ventures between competitors from the United States and Japan, Europe and Japan, and the United States and Europe. We did not judge the success or failure of each partnership by its longevity—a common mistake when evaluating strategic alliances—but by the shifts in competitive strength on each side. We focused on how companies use competitive collaboration to enhance their internal skills and technologies while they guard against transferring competitive advantages to ambitious partners.

There is no immutable law that strategic alliances *must* be a windfall for Japanese or Korean partners. Many Western companies do give away more than they gain—but that's because they enter partnerships without knowing what it takes to win. Companies that benefit most from competitive collaboration adhere to a set of simple but powerful principles.

Collaboration is competition in a different form. Successful companies never forget that their new partners may be out to disarm them. They enter alliances with clear strategic objectives, and they also understand how their partners' objectives will affect their success.

Harmony is not the most important measure of success. Indeed, occasional conflict may be the best evivendence of mutually beneficial collaboration. Few alliances remain win-win undertakings forever. A partner may be content even as it unknowingly surrenders core skills.

Cooperation has limits. Companies must defend against competitive compromise. A strategic alliance is a constantly evolving bargain whose real terms go beyond the legal agreement or the aims of top management. What information gets traded is determined day to day, often by engineers and operating managers.

It's not devious to absorb skills from your partner— that's the whole idea.

Successful companies inform employees at all levels about what skills and technologies are off-limits to the partner and monitor what the partner requests and receives.

Learning from partners is paramount. Successful companies view each alliance as a window on their partners' broad capabilities. They use the alliance to build skills in areas outside the formal agreement and systematically diffuse new knowledge throughout their organizations.

Why Collaborate?

Using an alliance with a competitor to acquire new technologies or skills is not devious. It reflects the commitment and capacity of each partner to absorb the skills of the other. We found that in every case in which a Japanese company emerged from an alliance stronger than its Western partner, the Japanese company had made a greater effort to learn.

Strategic intent is an essential ingredient in the commitment to learning. The willingness of Asian companies to enter alliances represents a change in competitive tactics, not competitive goals. NEC, for example, has used a series of collaborative ventures to enhance its technology and product competences. NEC is the only company in the world with a leading position in telecommunications, computers, and semiconductors—despite its investing less in R&D (as a percentage of revenues) than competitors like Texas Instruments, Northern Telecom, and L.M. Ericsson. Its string of partnerships, most notably with Honeywell, allowed NEC to leverage its in-house R&D over the last two decades.

Western companies, on the other hand, often enter alliances to avoid investments. They are more interested in reducing the costs and risks of entering new businesses or markets than in acquiring new skills. A senior U.S. manager offered this analysis of his company's venture with a Japanese rival: "We complement each other well—our distribution capability and their manufacturing skill. I see no reason to invest upstream if we can find a secure source of product. This is a comfortable relationship for us."

An executive from this company's Japanese partner offered a different perspective: "When it is necessary to collaborate, I go to my employees and say, 'This is bad, I wish we had these skills ourselves. Collaboration is second best. But I will feel worse if after four years we do not know how to do what our partner knows how to do.' We must digest their skills."

The problem here is not that the U.S. company wants to share investment risk (its Japanese partner does too) but that the U.S. company has no ambition *beyond* avoidance. When the commitment to learning is so one-sided, collaboration invariably leads to competitive compromise.

Many so-called alliances between Western companies and their Asian rivals are little more than sophisticated outsourcing arrangements (see "Competition for Competence" at the end of this article). General Motors buys cars and components from Korea's Daewoo. Siemens buys computers from Fujitsu. Apple buys laser printer engines from Canon. The traffic is almost entirely one way. These OEM deals offer Asian partners a way to capture investment initiative from Western competitors and displace customer-competitors from value-creating activities. In many cases this goal meshes with that of the Western partner: to regain competitiveness quickly and with minimum effort.

Consider the joint venture between Rover, the British automaker, and Honda. Some 25 years ago, Rover's forerunners were world leaders in small car design. Honda had not even entered the automobile business. But in the mid-1970s, after failing to penetrate foreign markets, Rover turned to Honda for technology and product-development support. Rover has used the alliance to avoid investments to design and build new cars. Honda has cultivated skills in European styling and marketing as well as multinational manufacturing. There is little doubt which company will emerge stronger over the long term.

Troubled laggards like Rover often strike alliances with surging latecomers like Honda. Having fallen behind in a key skills area (in this case, manufacturing small cars), the laggard attempts to compensate for past failures. The latecomer uses the alliance to close a specific skills gap (in this case, learning to build cars for a regional market). But a laggard that forges a partnership for short-term gain may find itself in a dependency spiral: as it contributes fewer and fewer distinctive skills, it must reveal more and more of its internal operations to keep the partner interested. For the weaker company, the issue shifts from "Should we collaborate?" to "With whom should we collaborate?" to "How do we keep our partner interested as we lose the advantages that made us attractive to them in the first place?"

There's a certain paradox here. When both partners are equally intent on internalizing the other's skills, distrust and conflict may spoil the alliance and threaten its very survival. That's one reason joint ventures between Korean and Japanese companies have been few and tempestuous. Neither side wants to "open the kimono." Alliances seem to run most smoothly when one partner is intent on learning and the other is intent on avoidance—in essence, when one partner is willing to grow dependent on the other. But running smoothly is not the point; the point is for a company to emerge from an alliance more competitive than when it entered it.

One partner does not always have to give up more than it gains to ensure the survival of an alliance. There are certain conditions under which mutual gain is possible, at least for a time:

The partners' strategic goals converge while their competitive goals diverge. That is, each partner allows for the other's continued prosperity in the shared business. Philips and Du Pont collaborate to develop and manufacture compact discs, but neither side invades the other's market. There is a clear upstream/downstream division of effort.

The size and market power of both partners is modest compared with industry leaders. This forces each side to accept that mutual dependence may have to continue for many years. Long-term collaboration may be so critical to both partners that neither will risk antagonizing the other by an overtly competitive bid to appropriate skills or competences. Fujitsu's 1 to 5 size disadvantage with IBM means it will be a long time, if ever, before Fujitsu can break away from its foreign partners and go it alone.

Each partner believes it can learn from the other and at the same time limit access to proprietary skills. JVC and Thomson, both of whom make VCRs, know that they are trading skills. But the two companies are looking for very different things. Thomson needs product technology and manufacturing prowess; JVC needs to learn how to succeed in the fragmented European market. Both sides believe there is an equitable chance for gain.

How to Build Secure Defenses

For collaboration to succeed, each partner must contribute something distinctive: basic research, product development skills, manufacturing capacity, access to distribution. The challenge is to share enough skills to create advantage vis-à-vis companies outside the alliance while preventing a wholesale transfer of core skills to the partner. This is a very thin line to walk. Companies must carefully select what skills and technologies they pass to their partners. They must develop safeguards against unintended, informal transfers of information. The goal is to limit the transparency of their operations.

The type of skill a company contributes is an important factor in how easily its partner can internalize the skills. The potential for transfer is greatest when a partner's contribution is easily transported (in engineering drawings, on computer tapes, or in the heads of a few technical experts); easily interpreted (it can be reduced to commonly understood equations or symbols); and easily absorbed (the skill or competence is independent of any particular cultural context).

Western companies face an inherent disadvantage because their skills are generally more vulnerable to transfer. The magnet that attracts so many companies to alliances with Asian competitors is their manufacturing excellence—a competence that is less transferable than most. Just-in-time inventory systems and quality circles can be imitated, but this is like pulling a few threads out of an oriental carpet. Manufacturing excellence is a complex web of employee training, integration with suppliers, statistical process controls, employee involvement, value engineering, and design for manufacture. It is difficult to extract such a subtle competence in any way but a piecemeal fashion.

There is an important distinction between technology and competence. A discrete, stand-alone technology (for example, the design of a semiconductor chip) is more easily transferred than a process competence, which is entwined in the social fabric of a company. Asian companies often learn more from their Western partners than vice versa because

Alliances should establish and enforce specific performance requirements. No performance, no technology transfer.

they contribute difficult-to-unravel strengths, while Western partners contribute easy-to-imitate technology.

So companies must take steps to limit transparency. One approach is to limit the scope of the formal agreement. It might cover a single technology rather than an entire range of technologies; part of a product line rather than the entire line; distribution in a limited number of markets or for a limited period of time. The objective is to circumscribe a partner's opportunities to learn.

Moreover, agreements should establish specific performance requirements. Motorola, for example, takes an incremental, incentive-based approach to technology transfer in its venture with Toshiba. The agreement calls for Motorola to release its microprocessor technology incrementally as Toshiba delivers on its promise to increase Motorola's penetration in the Japanese semiconductor market. The greater Motorola's market share, the greater Toshiba's access to Motorola's technology.

Many of the skills that migrate between companies are not covered in the formal terms of collaboration. Top management puts together strategic alliances and sets the legal parameters for exchange. But what actually gets traded is determined by day-to-day interactions of engineers, marketers, and product developers: who says what to whom, who gets access to what facilities, who sits on what joint committees. The most important deals ("I'll share this with you if you share that with me") may be struck four or five organizational levels below where the deal was signed. Here lurks the greatest risk of unintended transfers of important skills.

Consider one technology-sharing alliance between European and Japanese competitors. The European company valued the partnership as a way to acquire a specific technology. The Japanese company considered it a window on its partner's entire range of competences and interacted with a broad spectrum of its partner's marketing and product-development staff. The company mined each contact for as much information as possible.

For example, every time the European company requested a new feature on a product being sourced from its partner, the Japanese company asked for detailed customer and competitor analyses to justify the request. Over time, it developed a sophisticated picture of the European market that would assist its own entry strategy. The technology acquired by the European partner through the formal agreement had a useful life of three to five years. The competitive insights acquired informally by the Japanese company will probably endure longer.

Limiting unintended transfers at the operating level requires careful attention to the role of gatekeepers, the people who control what information flows to a partner. A gatekeeper can be effective only if there are a limited number of gateways through which a partner can access people and facilities. Fujitsu's many partners all go through a single office, the "collaboration section," to request information and assistance from different divisions. This way the company can monitor and control access to critical skills and technologies.

We studied one partnership between European and U.S. competitors that involved several divisions of each company. While the U.S. company could only access its partner through a single gateway, its partner had unfettered access to all participating divisions. The European company took advantage of its free rein. If one division refused to provide certain information, the European partner made the same request of another division. No single manager in the U.S. company could tell how much information had been transferred or was in a position to piece together patterns in the requests.

Collegiality is a prerequisite for collaborative success. But *too much* collegiality should set off warning bells to senior managers. CEOs or division presidents should expect occasional complaints from their counterparts about the reluctance of lower level employees to share information. That's a sign that the gatekeepers are doing their jobs. And senior management should regularly debrief operating personnel to find out what information the partner is requesting and what requests are being granted.

Limiting unintended transfers ultimately depends on employee loyalty and self-discipline. This was a real issue for many of the Western companies we studied. In their excitement and pride over technical achievements, engineering staffs sometimes shared information that top management considered sensitive. Japanese engineers were less likely to share proprietary information.

There are a host of cultural and professional reasons for the relative openness of Western technicians. Japanese engineers and scientists are more loyal to their company than to their profession. They are less steeped in the open give-and-take of university research since they receive much of their training from employers. They consider themselves team members more than individual scientific contributors.

When a foreign partner houses, feeds, and looks after your managers, there is a danger that they will "go native."

As one Japanese manager noted, "We don't feel any need to reveal what we know. It is not an issue of pride for us. We're glad to sit and listen. If we're patient we usually learn what we want to know."

Controlling unintended transfers may require restricting access to facilities as well as to people. Companies should declare sensitive laboratories and factories off-limits to their partners. Better yet, they might house the collaborative venture in an entirely new facility. IBM is building a special site in Japan where Fujitsu can review its forthcoming mainframe software before deciding whether to license it. IBM will be able to control exactly what Fujitsu sees and what information leaves the facility.

Finally, which country serves as "home" to the alliance affects transparency. If the collaborative team is located near one partner's major facilities, the other partner will have more opportunities to learn—but less control over what information gets traded. When the partner houses, feeds, and looks after engineers and operating managers, there is a danger they will "go native." Expatriate personnel need frequent visits from headquarters as well as regular furloughs home.

"Our Western partners approach us with the attitude of teachers. We have the attitude of students."

Enhance the Capacity to Learn

Whether collaboration leads to competitive surrender or revitalization depends foremost on what employees believe the purpose of the alliance to be. It is self-evident: to learn, one must *want* to learn. Western companies won't realize the full benefits of competitive collaboration until they overcome an arrogance borne of decades of leadership. In short, Western companies must be more receptive.

We asked a senior executive in a Japanese electronics company about the perception that Japanese companies learn more from their foreign partners than vice versa.

"Our Western partners approach us with the attitude of teachers," he told us. "We are quite happy with this, because we have the attitude of students."

Learning begins at the top. Senior management must be committed to enhancing their companies' skills as well as to avoiding financial risk. But most learning takes place at the lower levels of an alliance. Operating employees not only represent the front lines in an effective defense but also play a vital role in acquiring knowledge. They must be well briefed on the partner's strengths and weaknesses and understand how acquiring particular skills will bolster their company's competitive position.

This is already standard practice among Asian companies. We accompanied a Japanese development engineer on a tour through a partner's factory. This engineer dutifully took notes on plant layout, the number of production stages, the rate at which the line was running, and the number of employees. He recorded all this despite the fact that he had no manufacturing responsibility in his own company, and that the alliance didn't encompass joint manufacturing. Such dedication greatly enhances learning.

Collaboration doesn't always provide an opportunity to fully internalize a partner's skills. Yet just acquiring new and more precise benchmarks of a partner's performance can be of great value. A new benchmark can provoke a thorough review of internal performance levels and may spur a round of competitive innovation. Asking questions like, "Why do their semiconductor logic designs have fewer errors than ours?" and "Why are they investing in this technology and we're not?" may provide the incentive for a vigorous catch-up program.

Competitive benchmarking is a tradition in most of the Japanese companies we studied. It requires many of the same skills associated with competitor analysis: systematically calibrating performance against external targets; learning to use rough estimates to determine where a competitor (or partner) is better, faster, or cheaper; translating those estimates into new internal targets; and recalibrating to establish the rate of improvement in a competitor's performance. The great advantage of competitive collaboration is that proximity makes benchmarking easier.

Indeed, some analysts argue that one of Toyota's motivations in collaborating with GM in the much-publicized NUMMI venture is to gauge the quality of GM's manufacturing technology. GM's top manufacturing people get a close look at Toyota, but the reverse is true as well. Toyota may be learning whether its giant U.S. competitor is capable of closing the productivity gap with Japan.

Competitive collaboration also provides a way of getting close enough to rivals to predict how they will behave when the alliance unravels or runs its course. How does the partner respond to price changes? How does it measure and reward executives? How does it prepare to launch a new product? By revealing a competitor's management orthodoxies, collaboration can increase the chances of success in future head-to-head battles.

Knowledge acquired from a competitor-partner is only valuable after it is diffused through the organization. Several companies we studied had established internal clearinghouses to collect and disseminate information. The collaborations manager at one Japanese company regularly made the rounds of all employees involved in alliances. He identified what information had been collected by whom and then passed it on to appropriate departments. Another company held regular meetings where employees shared new knowledge and determined who was best positioned to acquire additional information.

Proceed with Care—But Proceed

After World War II, Japanese and Korean companies entered alliances with Western rivals from weak positions. But they worked steadfastly toward independence. In the early 1960s, NEC's computer business was one-quarter the size of Honeywell's, its primary foreign partner. It took only two decades for NEC to grow larger than Honeywell, which eventually sold its computer operations to an alliance between NEC and Groupe Bull of France. The NEC experience demonstrates that dependence on a foreign partner doesn't automatically condemn a company to also-ran status. Collaboration may sometimes be unavoidable; surrender is not.

Managers are too often obsessed with the ownership structure of an alliance. Whether a company controls 51% or 49% of a joint venture may be much less important than the rate at which each partner learns from the other. Companies that are confident in their ability to learn may even prefer some ambiguity in the alliance's legal structure. Ambiguity creates more potential to acquire skills and technologies. The challenge for Western companies is not to write tighter legal agreements but to become better learners.

Running away from collaboration is no answer. Even the largest Western companies can no longer outspend their global rivals. With leadership in many industries shifting toward the East, companies in the United States and Europe must become good borrowers—much like Asian companies did in the 1960s and 1970s. Competitive renewal depends on building new process capabilities and winning new product and technology battles. Collaboration can be a low-cost strategy for doing both.

About Our Research

WE SPENT MORE THAN five years studying the internal workings of 15 strategic alliances around the world. We sought answers to a series of interrelated questions. What role have strategic alliances and outsourcing agreements played in the global success of Japanese and Korean companies? How do alliances change the competitive balance between partners? Does winning at collaboration mean different things to different companies? What factors determine who gains most from collaboration?

To understand who won and who lost and why, we observed the interactions of the partners first-hand and at multiple levels in each organization. Our sample included four European-U.S. alliances, two intra-European alliances, two European-Japanese alliances, and seven U.S.-Japanese alliances. We gained access to both sides of the partnerships in about half the cases and studied each alliance for an average of three years.

Confidentiality was a paramount concern. Where we did have access to both sides, we often wound up knowing more about who was doing what to whom than either of the partners. To preserve confidentiality, our article disguises many of the alliances that were part of the study.

Competition for Competence

IN THE ARTICLE "Do You Really Have a Global Strategy?" (HBR July–August 1985), Gary Hamel and C.K. Prahalad examined one dimension of the global competitive battle: the race for brand dominance. This is the battle for control of distribution channels and global "share of mind." Another global battle has been much less visible and has received much less management attention.This is the battle for control over key technology-based competences that fuel new business development.

Honda has built a number of businesses, including marine engines, lawn mowers, generators, motorcycles, and cars, around its engine and power train competence. Casio draws on its expertise in semiconductors and digital display in producing calculators, small-screen televisions, musical instruments, and watches. Canon relies on its imaging and microprocessor competences in its camera, copier, and laser printer businesses

In the short run, the quality and performance of a company's products determine its competitiveness. Over the longer term, however, what counts is the ability to build and enhance core competences—distinctive skills that spawn new generations of products. This is where many managers and commentators fear Western companies are losing. Our research helps explain why some companies may be more likely than others to surrender core skills.

Alliance or Outsourcing?

Enticing Western companies into outsourcing agreements provides several benefits to ambitious OEM partners. Serving as a manufacturing base for a Western partner is a quick route to increased manufacturing share without the risk or expense of building brand share. The Western partners' distribution capability allows Asian suppliers to focus all their resources on building absolute product advantage. Then OEMs can enter markets on their own and convert manufacturing share into brand share.

Serving as a sourcing platform yields more than just volume and process improvements. It also generates low-cost, low-risk market learning. The downstream (usually Western) partner typically provides information on how to tailor products to local markets. So every product design transferred to an OEM partner is also a research report on customer preferences and market needs. The OEM partner can use these insights to read the market accurately when it enters on its own.

A Ratchet Effect

Our research suggests that once a significant sourcing relationship has been established, the buyer becomes less willing and able to reemerge as a manufacturing competitor. Japanese and Korean companies are, with few exceptions, exemplary suppliers. If anything, the "soft option" of outsourcing becomes even softer as OEM suppliers routinely exceed delivery and quality expectations.

Outsourcing often begins a ratchetlike process. Relinquishing manufacturing control and paring back plant investment leads to sacrifices in product design, process technology, and, eventually, R&D budgets. Consequently, the OEM partner captures product-development as well as manufacturing initiative. Ambitious OEM partners are not content with the old formula of "You design it and we'll make it." The new reality is, "You design it, we'll learn from your designs, make them more manufacturable, and launch our products alongside yours."

Reversing the Verdict

This outcome is not inevitable. Western companies can retain control over their core competences by keeping a few simple principles in mind.

A competitive product is not the same thing as a competitive organization. While an Asian OEM partner may provide the former, it seldom provides the latter. In essence, outsourcing is a way of renting someone else's competitiveness rather than developing a long-term solution to competitive decline.

Rethink the make-or-buy decision. Companies often treat component manufacturing operations as cost centers and transfer their output to assembly units at an arbitrarily set price. This transfer price is an accounting fiction, and it is unlikely to yield as high a return as marketing or distribution investments, which require less research money and capital. But companies seldom consider the competitive consequences of surrendering control over a key value-creating activity.

Watch out for deepening dependence. Surrender results from a series of outsourcing decisions that individually make economic sense but collectively amount to a phased exit from the business. Different managers make outsourcing decisions at different times, unaware of the cumulative impact.

Replenish core competences. Western companies must outsource some activities; the economics are just too compelling. The real issue is whether a company is adding to its stock of technologies and competences as rapidly as it is surrendering them. The question of whether to outsource should always provoke a second question: Where can we outpace our partner and other rivals in building new sources of competitive advantage?

Notes

1. For a vigorous warning about the perils of collaboration, see Robert B. Reich and Eric D. Mankin, "Joint Ventures with Japan Give Away Our Future," HBR March–April 1986, p. 78.

Originally published in January–February 1989
Reprint 89104

Is Your Strategic Alliance Really a Sale?

JOEL BLEEKE AND DAVID ERNST

Executive Summary

INCREASINGLY, SENIOR EXECUTIVES who wish to expand their company's product, geographic, or customer reach consider alliances to be the strategic vehicle of choice. In the past five years, the number of domestic and cross-border alliances has grown by more than 25% annually. But the term *alliance* can be deceptive: in many cases, it really means an eventual transfer of ownership. The median life span for alliances is only about seven years, and nearly 80% of joint ventures end in a sale by one of the partners.

It's dangerous to ignore these statistics. If a CEO does not realize that an alliance will probably end in a sale, he or she may be betting the company without knowing it. If the endgame is not anticipated, what begins as a strategic partnership can lead to an unplanned sale that erodes shareholder value.

However, an alliance can be a good acquisition or divestiture vehicle if its evolution is planned. Such evaluation can help companies avoid disastrous partnerships. It can help managers choose corporate partners that will advance their organization's long-term strategic plan. And it can help reveal opportunities in which an alliance may be used as a low-risk, low-cost option on a future acquisition.

Based on the authors' experience with more than 200 alliances in various stages, they have developed a way for managers to diagnose whether an alliance is likely to lead to a sale and to devise an appropriate strategy—to assess bargaining positions and the risks of unplanned outcomes, and to plan for the partnership's evolution. They distinguish six types of alliances based on their probable outcomes: collisions between competitors, alliances of the weak, disguised sales, bootstrap alliances, evolutions to a sale, and alliances of complementary equals.

INCREASINGLY, SENIOR EXECUTIVES who wish to expand their company's product, geographic, or customer reach consider alliances to be the strategic vehicle of choice. In the past five years, the number of domestic and cross-border alliances has grown by more than 25% annually. But the term *alliance* can be deceptive; in many cases, an alliance really means an eventual transfer of ownership. The median life span for alliances is only about seven years, and nearly 80% of joint ventures—one of the most common alliance structures—ultimately end in a sale by one of the partners.

It's dangerous to ignore the trend. If a CEO does not realize that an alliance will probably end in a sale, he or she may be betting the company without knowing it. If the endgame is not anticipated, what begins as a strategic partnership can lead to an unplanned sale that erodes shareholder value. What's more, since an alliance does not generally receive the same intense public scrutiny that an acquisition or a divestiture does, the board and shareholders may also be unaware of the true risk.

By contrast, an alliance can be a good acquisition or divestiture vehicle if its evolution is planned. That's why thinking through whether an alliance might lead to a sale is critical. Such evaluation can help companies avoid disastrous partnerships and unanticipated sales of important businesses. It can help managers choose corporate partners that will advance their organization's long-term strategic plan. And it can help reveal opportunities in which an alliance may be used as a low-risk, low-cost option on a future acquisition.

Based on our experience with more than 200 alliances in various phases from initial negotiations through termination, we have developed a way for managers to diagnose whether an alliance is likely to lead to a sale and to devise an appropriate strategy—to assess bargaining positions and the risks of unplanned outcomes, and to plan for the partnership's evolution. The alliances we've studied span a broad range of industry and service sectors and include 49 strategic partnerships between some of the largest companies in the United States, Europe, and Asia that we have tracked

Alliances between competitors with similar core businesses, markets, and skills tend to fail.

since 1989. Although our experience base includes many types of alliances, this article focuses mostly on situations in which both or all companies bring major business interests to the deal, a separate entity is created (for example, a joint venture), and the partners share risks and financial rewards.

Avoiding Self-Deception

The reason senior managers may not take the time to think through the evolution of a planned alliance is that they may already believe they have their company's long-term interests well in hand. They may think their reasons for forging an alliance are grounded in the strongest of strategies. But, caught up in the thrill of the chase or the intensity of negotiations, many managers deceive themselves. If you find yourself uttering one of the following statements, beware! Your alliance may lead your company toward an unplanned divestiture.

"We're better off partnering with X than competing against it in our core business." The strategic flaw here is using "acquisition thinking" rather than "partnership thinking"—choosing partners that are direct competitors rather than complementary allies. Alliances between competitors with similar core businesses, geographic markets, and functional skills tend to fail because of tensions between the partners. Conflicts emerge or intensify as both parties expand into the same markets. In fact, the success rate for alliances involving potentially overlapping core-product markets is only about one in three. (We consider an alliance successful if both parties achieve their strategic objectives and earn a return equal to or greater than their cost of capital over the life of the partnership.)

"By joining forces with another second-tier company, we can create a strong company while fixing our problems together." The idea that two weak companies can combine to form a strong unit is appealing, but such ventures usually fail to strengthen the position of either partner. Instead, the alliance sinks because of the very weaknesses it was supposed to fix. Even worse, should one or both of the corporate parents decide to divest, the partnership can complicate a sale.

"We need a strong partner to improve our skills." Alliances can and should be regarded as opportunities for organizational learning. But when the primary purpose of a partnership is for the weaker company to improve its skills, the venture will usually fail. In such cases, the top-level managers involved have generally not paid enough attention to the business logic of the deal—that is, how the partnership will create value. Often, the partner seeking to learn is unable to contribute sufficiently to the alliance.

"By partnering with another company in our industry, we can access its new products and technologies while minimizing our investments in core products and technologies." This mind-set is common in globalizing industries such as telecommunications, computers, and airlines—or wherever weaker players face declining market share and profitability because of new, low-cost competitors. But using an alliance to compete in scale-driven industries can be a recipe for disaster, especially if the company is trying to replace products or technologies that are critical to its core business. Over time, the

The key to understanding whether an alliance is likely to lead to a sale is to project how bargaining power will evolve.

weaker company is rarely able to match the stronger company in creating new technologies and products, and the imbalance typically leads to a sale, often for little or no acquisition premium.

"We can use an alliance to raise capital without giving up management control." A venture based on this premise works only if one of the partners is a largely passive investor that does not seek involvement in the business in return for its financial stake. In industries as diverse as biotechnology and steel, when a manager looks to a partner for capital, the deal tends to be unbalanced from the start. In effect, the weaker partner sells its capabilities in return for capital. Moreover, that partner is generally forced to reduce its stake over time because the stronger partner must fund future investments.

Assessing Risks

The key to understanding whether an alliance is likely to lead to a sale—and which company is the likely buyer—is to project how the relative bargaining power of the partners will evolve. Relative bargaining power depends on three factors: the initial strengths and weaknesses of the partners, how those strengths and weaknesses change over time, and the potential for competitive conflict.

INITIAL STRENGTHS AND WEAKNESSES

Ask yourself the following questions: What specific business strengths—such as products, technologies, market access, and functional skills—does each partner have, and which of those elements is most important for the venture's long-term success in the marketplace (for example, blockbuster drugs in pharmaceutical alliances)? Which partner controls the customers that will be served by the venture? Which company will fill more of the venture's top management positions? Which partner is more able and willing to invest in the alliance, based on profitability, cash on hand, and the strategic importance of the business?

Those starting positions determine the value of the bargaining chips that each partner brings to the table. When the balance of power is tilted from the start, the stronger partner is usually the eventual owner. In the alliance between Meiji Milk Products and Borden to sell premium dairy products in Japan, Meiji originally controlled the relationships with the retail outlets, and Borden supplied the products. When the partnership was phased out between 1990 and 1992, Meiji retained control of the distribution and manufacturing facilities and introduced its own products in the premium ice cream, cheese, and margarine segments. Borden subsequently exited the Japanese market after its sales and market share declined.

HOW STRENGTHS CHANGE OVER TIME

Even if bargaining power is balanced at the outset of an alliance, strengths may change within a few years, creating a massive shift in bargaining power and leading to an unanticipated sale. In the initial stages of industry development, for example, the product and technology provider generally has the most power. But unless those products and technologies are proprietary and unique, power usually shifts to the party that controls distribution channels and customers. And if the industry becomes a scale-driven commodity business, the key to success becomes process-design capabilities. Consider what happened to a U.S. chemicals company—a world-class producer of industrial coatings—that formed an alliance with a Japanese organization. After a few highly successful years of alliance, the Japanese company proposed a buyout. It had learned the production-process skills originally supplied by the U.S. organization, and it still controlled the relationships with key customers. The U.S. company had no choice but to divest.

Other factors also contribute to shifts in power. For one, partners that put most of the senior managers into the key functions of an alliance are likely to see their strength grow even if they start out as shareholders with a minority equity stake. For another, the ability to invest in an alliance over time often becomes increasingly important after the deal is done; the parent that invests more usually gets greater decision-making power and an increased equity stake. The parent's relative capacity (and appetite) to invest is especially important because alliances generally require more capital than planned for: if the alliance is successful, capital is needed to expand; if it underperforms, capital is needed to meet shortfalls in cash flow.

Finally, bargaining power is strongly affected by the balance of learning and teaching in an alliance. A company that is good at learning—and that structures the alliance in such a way that it can access and internalize its partner's capabilities—is likely to become less dependent on its partner as the alliance evolves.

POTENTIAL FOR COMPETITIVE CONFLICT

When direct competitors whose product and geographic positions overlap try to forge an alliance, conflict is inevitable. Often the parties will reach a stalemate on important issues, such as which markets to target, which products and customers to emphasize, or whose factory to close. To resolve the conflicts and capture the benefits of scale in such cases, the partners usually move toward complete integration by a full merger or an acquisition—or they simply dissolve the alliance.

It's critical to know which of six paths and alliance is on: all but one risk an unanticipated sale.

In contrast, the potential for competitive conflict and the risk of an unanticipated sale are minimal when each partner brings distinctive qualities to the table—for example, different geographic, product, and functional positions. When each company builds on the other's qualities rather than trying to fill gaps in core businesses or markets, the venture's strengths together equal more than the sum of the parts. Pepsico and Lipton, for example, have combined their very different strengths to produce and market canned iced tea. Lipton brings its expertise in the tea business; Pepsico brings access to beverage distribution channels. In theory, Pepsico could provide the product, but Lipton has built the franchise and brand awareness that it needs to retain significant control over customers. Bargaining power thus remains balanced; the alliance can endure because each partner controls its own turf.

Managing the Risks of an Evolving Alliance

By analyzing initial strengths, how they change, and the potential for competitive conflict, it is possible to map a particular alliance and anticipate or protect against a future sale of the business. We've found that alliances generally fall into one of six categories, which we've named based on their probable outcomes: collisions between competitors, alliances of the weak, disguised sales, bootstrap alliances, evolutions to a sale, and alliances of complementary equals. It's critical to know which of those paths an alliance is on because all but one carry the risk of an unanticipated sale, which can be a major blunder for the partner that ends up divesting. (See "Seller Beware" at the end of this article.)

In fact, the first two types—collisions between competitors and alliances of the weak—almost always fail and should be avoided. The next two—disguised sales and bootstrap alliances—pair strong companies with weak companies, and, although they are risky and usually result in a sale, they can benefit both partners if properly structured and managed. The last two—evolutions to a sale and alliances of complementary equals—pair strong companies with strong companies, but only the latter generally lead to ventures that are both successful and enduring. We'll describe all six types in detail.

COLLISIONS BETWEEN COMPETITORS

Managers typically choose direct competitors as partners because such alliances tend to create great short-term synergy through consolidation of overlapping product and market positions. The illusory attraction of an alliance as opposed to an acquisition is that control can be shared with neither party giving up power, while the synergy can be captured and split between each one. But when both partners want to expand their core businesses based on the same set of geographic and product opportunities, conflict is the rule, not the exception.

For example, take the joint venture formed by a U.S. company and an Asian competitor to market point-of-sale terminals in the United States. The partnership led rapidly to conflicts over how to tailor and sell the Asian partner's products in the U.S. market. The partners, both selling their own point-of-sale terminals in the United States through the joint venture, couldn't resolve those issues, and the venture reportedly lost as much as $20 million annually. After three unprofitable years, the Asian partner bought out the U.S. partner's 49% stake to gain control over decision making. With the conflicts resolved, the Asian partner was able to increase the unit's performance, achieving a reported market share of more than 20% in target segments.

Another example is the alliance between General Electric and Rolls-Royce in jet engines, which ended in 1986 amid charges that Rolls-Royce had introduced a directly competitive engine. The lesson is that direct competitors with a high degree of overlap tend to be among the worst alliance partners. Managers should consider either acquiring such competitors or partnering with companies that focus on different businesses or geographic markets.

ALLIANCES OF THE WEAK

In this kind of partnership, two or more weak companies band together in the hope that their combined forces will improve their positions. Generally, however, the weak grow weaker and the alliance fails. Often a third party acquires the pieces.

The bottom line: if you can't succeed on your own, an alliance with another weak company won't make things any better. Unfortunately, many clusters of alliances are being driven by weakness, not strength. The airline industry provides a telling example. By the early 1990s, alliances had proliferated among players in this globalizing industry. Yet many of the deals involved linkages between weak players—for example, unprofitable U.S. airlines and flag carriers of smaller European countries. Many of these investments have already resulted in significant write-offs, and several alliances have unraveled.

Alliances of the weak often begin when weak companies join to try to compete in scale-intensive businesses. But when things get rough—as our research shows is often the case in the first three years of any alliance—neither partner has the requisite capital, management resources, or flexibility to provide much help. Usually, the demands for scale—and capital—outpace the abilities of weak partners to invest, and they are too busy trying to fix their core business to devote sufficient attention to managing their partnership.

When the time comes to call it quits, the logical next step is to try to sell to a stronger company with the resources to effect a turnaround. But many companies trying to divest after an alliance has been formed realize much less value than if they had conducted an outright sale in the first place. Potential buyers are often deterred by the difficulty of dissolving an alliance; what's more, competitive assets—skills, customers, and products—may have eroded in the interim. A better strategy for a weak company is to divest outright or to refocus the business and then think about an alliance.

DISGUISED SALES

In this type of alliance, a weak company joins a strong company that either is or will be directly competitive. Usually the weaker player remains weak and is acquired by the stronger player. Such ventures tend to be short-lived, rarely lasting more than five years.

In the real world, alliances are frequently pursued as a second-best strategy when management is unwilling to sell a weak company. Yet shareholders usually would be better off if the company were sold at the outset. When weak companies believe they must hook up with a strong company, they need to recognize the risk that the alliance will end up as an acquisition. Such an awareness requires "divestiture thinking," not "alliance thinking."

For starters, potential sellers should seek partners that would be the best buyers later on. Those partners are more likely to be potential competitors than complementary partners, because direct competitors are best able to maximize synergy. They should have ample cash for investment and acquisition. In the Siemens/Allis-Chalmers venture in power equipment (Siemens Allis Power Engineering), Siemens viewed the business as a core strategic area, had strong technology, was willing to invest, and wanted to expand in the United States. Allis-Chalmers had distribution, sales, and manufacturing capabilities but limited capital to invest in developing new technologies and products. Given that combination, says one Siemens executive, it was no surprise that "in the back of everyone's mind was the notion that when and if the venture ended, Siemens would be the likely buyer." By 1982, four years after the alliance was formed, Siemens had raised its stake to 85%. The full buyout occurred in 1985. Siemens subsequently made additional acquisitions to build a business with more than $1 billion in U.S. sales.

It is also critical for sellers to recognize that their bargaining power will decline over time and to negotiate explicit exit provisions that ensure fair value in the event of a sale. Those provisions must lock in the value (or the formula for calculating it) at the outset. The usual approach—delaying negotiations about valuation until a sale is imminent—is not sufficient to protect the weaker company's shareholders, because bargaining power is likely to shift to the stronger company over time.

Allis-Chalmers realized the importance of exit clauses in its joint venture with Siemens. According to Hans W. Decker, a former vice chairman of Siemens in the United States, "The exit clause, which specified that Siemens had the right to acquire the venture at a specific pricing formula in the event of termination, was the most important item in the agreement. If we talked about the joint venture agreement for three months, we talked about the exit clause for two months." In another case, when a company in the industrial-coatings business formed a joint venture with a likely buyer, they negotiated a buy-sell price in advance based on the initial value of the business plus 50% of the synergies that they estimated would result.

When a sale is likely, the alliance should be structured so that the business that is to be sold is easily separated. In the Siemens/Allis-Chalmers joint venture, Siemens created a stand-alone entity by locating the alliance's headquarters in Atlanta, Georgia, rather than Milwaukee, Wisconsin, where Allis-Chalmers was based. The idea is to define clear boundaries for the venture relative to the parent organizations in terms of the assets, activities, and people that will be involved. The fewer remaining entanglements (such as

We generally advise against entering into a bootstrap alliance unless it is impossible to fix or sell the business.

transfer pricing arrangements for services provided by the parents), the easier the sale.

BOOTSTRAP ALLIANCES

This type of alliance is often tried but rarely works. A weak company partners with a stronger (and often complementary) company and attempts to use the alliance to improve its capabilities. For the weaker partner, this strategy is the equivalent of drawing to an inside straight in poker. Usually the weak partner remains weak and is acquired by the stronger partner. In the few cases where the strategy succeeds, the partnership develops into an alliance of equals or the partners separate after the weak partner has become able to compete on its own.

We generally advise against this strategy unless it is impossible to fix or sell the business. Making a bootstrap alliance work is a daunting task: it entails a systematic learning program and the ability to learn; a partner with the right skills that is willing to teach and will not become an acquirer; and a window of several years to execute the strategy. One example of a successful bootstrap alliance is that between Rover and Honda. Rover began as an unprofitable state-owned enterprise and improved to the point where British Aerospace, Rover's parent, could sell 80% of the unit to BMW for £800 million (about $1.2 billion). Could British Aerospace have sold Rover for a similar sum without the capability building that the alliance allowed? We doubt it. But through the alliance, Rover increased its productivity, cut its defect rate by more than half, and reduced its product development cycle from six and a half to four and a half years.

Weak partners entering a bootstrap alliance must recognize that the deal may lead to a sale and that the stronger partner will have more bargaining power. Therefore, like weak partners in disguised sales, they should structure exit provisions to ensure fair value in the event of a divestiture.

The design of the partnership is also crucial in a bootstrap alliance. Weak partners should structure the deal so that they retain control over one or more major business elements, like customer relationships. They should also ensure that the capability gaps are limited to a few key areas.

In addition, weak partners should consider designing the alliance around a series of skill-building activities. And the structure of the deal should support the learning agenda. For example, Thomson Consumer Electronics of France, in its alliance with JVC, sought to improve its skills in the precision manufacturing and assembly required to produce high-quality VCRs. (The alliance was initially formed in 1982 by JVC, Thorn EMI of the United Kingdom, and Telefunken of Germany. Thomson subsequently purchased Telefunken, and Thorn divested its stake in the venture to Thomson and JVC.) An important early step for Thomson was to identify a series of discrete, achievable steps to build its capabilities. First, it focused on developing assembly skills. Then its efforts graduated to manufacturing components, manufacturing complete VCRs, and later, building capabilities necessary for designing and producing a new VCR model.[1]

In this case, JVC licensed its designs to the joint venture, which had significant manufacturing facilities in Germany and the United Kingdom. JVC committed to increasing the value of VCR components produced by the joint venture in Europe and to assisting Thomson in setting up and managing a separate Thomson-owned component-and-subsystem supply plant in France. Most of the joint venture's employees were from Thomson, and workers in the Berlin plant were rotated to nearby Thomson production lines to promote skills transfer. Government protection can also increase the chances of success for the weaker partner in a bootstrap alliance, especially if stronger companies are forced to transfer technology to gain access to the market. For example, U.S. telecommunications companies are generally prohibited from outright acquisitions in Eastern Europe, allowing Eastern European telecommunications players to build their networks and capabilities without the risk of an unwanted acquisition.

EVOLUTIONS TO A SALE

These alliances start with two strong and compatible partners, but competitive tensions may develop or bargaining power may shift, and one partner ultimately sells out to the other. However, such partnerships often deliver value to both parties and may exceed the seven-year average life span for alliances.

Sometimes power is so evenly balanced at the outset that these ventures may appear to be alliances of complementary equals, and it can be difficult to tell which partner is likely to emerge as a buyer. Neither partner, for example, may know enough initially to manage the business alone even if it could buy it. There usually are clues, however, that indicate how bargaining power may shift. The key is to examine what business strengths each partner plans to contribute, which partner supplies most of the senior managers, which is willing to invest more, and how the ratio of learning to teaching is likely to unfold. For example, take two large and equally successful pharmaceutical companies that formed a joint venture to distribute a specific product in the United States. The alliance lasted ten years yet was clearly perceived as an evolution to a sale, even in the beginning, because one of the partners held the key product patents. And, in fact, that partner did eventually buy out the other, following the terms of a predetermined buyout clause.

Industry evolution can also provide some insights: if a company is in an industry in which power is shifting from products to customers or core processes, and that company provides the products, the alliance may very well be an evolution to the company's sale.

Because these alliances are based on initially balanced contributions and can last a long time, they require a different approach to structuring than the alliances we've discussed. First, the partners should share an interest in structuring reciprocal and fair exit provisions that protect each one's strategic and financial interests. It is more important to devise formulas for dividing the future value of the venture fairly than it is to protect each partner's initial contribution.

Second, the partners should structure the alliance so that the contributions made and the value received are reviewed regularly and an appropriate balance is maintained. For example, Honeywell typically builds in sunset clauses to force renegotiation of its alliances every five years or so. Flexibility can be enhanced if the partners agree on the underlying principles for resolving conflicts and agree to honor them if the technical or legal arrangements prove to be unfair. Flexibility is also needed to allow partners to broaden or narrow the scope of the alliance to meet market requirements or to resolve any conflicts that might emerge.

Third, partners in evolutions to a sale need to be clear about their strategic intent. If one party wishes to be the eventual buyer if the venture ends up as a sale, the initial structure should reflect that desire. Would-be buyers need to invest heavily in the venture—with both people and capital. They also should make sure that the alliance allows for a favorable balance between learning and teaching. In the 1950s, for example, U.S.-based Pfizer formed a fifty-fifty joint venture with Taito, Japan's leading sugar producer, to enter the Japanese pharmaceutical market. Taito provided a Japanese beachhead, but Pfizer retained the patents on key drugs. Over time, Pfizer built up its own knowledge of the Japanese pharmaceutical market and eventually bought out the venture, becoming one of the largest foreign pharmaceutical companies in Japan.

One interesting note: many U.S.-Japanese alliances are evolutions to a sale, and generally the Japanese partners become the buyers. A study of joint ventures in Japan by McKinsey & Company's Tokyo office indicated that two-thirds of the ventures between Japanese and foreign companies operating in Japan had been sold to the Japanese partner upon termination. In part, that is because Japanese companies tend to focus more closely on absorbing their partner's capabilities.

Japanese companies are also more likely to acquire their ventures because their primary reasons for entering into alliances are strategic, not financial. When we surveyed 90 executives from 25 large Japanese companies, the vast majority (more than 80%) indicated that gaining the skills to enter new businesses and improving the strategic position of existing businesses were the main reasons for forming strategic alliances.

ALLIANCES OF COMPLEMENTARY EQUALS

This partnership path is the only one that can lead to a marriage for life. It involves two strong and complementary partners, and both generally remain strong for the duration. These alliances almost always last much longer than 7 years. In fact, the hallmark of such ventures is that neither partner could (or would rationally wish to) buy and manage the business. Dow Corning is more than 50 years old, Fuji Xerox is more than 30, and Siecor—an alliance between Siemens and Corning—is more than 15.

Such alliances are based on true collaboration in which both partners build on each other's qualities rather than trying to fill gaps. Often the partners have different product, geographic, or functional strengths. (See the exhibit, "Combining Complementary Strengths Creates Value.")

In the Siecor alliance, Siemens and Corning brought together their complementary capabilities in telecommunications and glass technology to build an indepen-

Combining Complementary Strengths Creates Value

Partner *Strength...* +	Partner *Strength...* =	Joint Objective
Pepsico *marketing clout for canned beverages*	**Lipton** *recognized tea brand and customer franchise*	To sell canned iced tea beverages jointly
KFC *established brand and store format, and operations skills*	**Mitsubishi** *real estate and site-selection skills in Japan*	To establish a KFC chain in Japan
Siemens *presence in range of telecommunications markets worldwide and cable-manufacturing technology*	**Corning** *technological strength in optical fibers and glass*	To create a fiber-optic-cable business
Ericsson *technological strength in public telecommunications networks*	**Hewlett-Packard** *computers, software, and access to electronics channels*	To create and market network management systems

dent joint venture that has gained a leadership position in the fiber-optic-cable business. Because both partners see the alliance as an important and profitable business, neither has desired to exit it. Both hold important patents on which the venture relies, so their bargaining power has remained relatively equal, and the risk of an unplanned divestiture is low.

In alliances of complementary equals, governance is critical. While the initial contract must be solid to get the venture off to a good start, it is not the key to success, because the terms of the deal usually change so much over time. The real challenges are to build in flexibility, maintain the balance of contributions, and ensure clarity of leadership. If governance is well planned and managed, the alliance will promote independence, fairness, and trust; each partner will prosper under equal equity ownership. And, as with all alliance types, the exit provisions should be carefully thought out—just in case. Managers should focus on assessing the future value of each company's stake and of the alliance as a whole: if the partnership is successful, the initial values will soon become obsolete.

Ultimately, the challenge in all alliances is to decide whether to try to keep the strengths and contributions in balance or to accept that the balance of power will inevitably shift and to plan accordingly. Failing to ask the right questions before closing a deal can lead to one of the worst decisions a manager can make: committing to an unanticipated sale of the business—often without prior board approval and for far less than the business would fetch in an open auction. In the heat of negotiations, rolling an alliance forward to examine its evolution may seem like a distraction. But given the high stakes, it is well worth the time and effort.

Seller Beware

TO UNDERSTAND THE POTENTIAL disadvantage of selling a company after it already has become part of an alliance, consider the seller's position in a straightforward acquisition. The seller gets paid for 100% of the business on day one. What's more, if a number of potential buyers are vying for the company in a competitive public auction, as is often the case, the eventual winner generally pays the seller a premium of as much as 50%. The seller's shareholders clearly benefit.

By contrast, consider the situation the seller faces in an alliance setting. An alliance partner that becomes the ultimate buyer has intimate involvement and knowledge of the business, and can estimate the likely synergies that will come from the acquisition with much greater confidence. In contrast to the buyer in a straightforward acquisition, who pays for the full business on day one, an alliance buyer often gets to defer paying for the business until the end of the alliance. Potential buyers can also limit their financial risk by structuring the partnership in such a way that they have an option to terminate it, such as a put option to exit the alliance after a trial period in which they can assess the value of their partner.

As a result, many companies that wind up selling the business to an alliance partner are unable to capture the full value of the business for their shareholders. Because the buyer's bargaining power tends to increase over the course of the partnership, the buyer often gets the lion's share of the synergies from the alliance without having to pay a full acquisition premium. Other potential buyers are likely to be deterred by the difficulty of unwinding the alliance, so the seller is usually unable to orchestrate a bidding process to drive up the acquisition price.

The Six Types of Alliances

Collisions Between Competitors

These alliances involve the core business of two strong companies that are direct competitors. Because of competitive tensions, they tend to be short-lived and fail to achieve their strategic and financial goals. Most collisions between competitors end in dissolution, acquisition by one of the partners, or a merger.

Alliances of the Weak

Two or more weak companies join forces, hoping that together they will improve their positions. But the weak usually grow weaker and the alliance fails, followed quickly by dissolution or acquisition by a third party.

Disguised Sales

In these partnerships, a weak company combines with a strong company, often one that is or will become directly competitive. The weaker player remains weak and is acquired by the stronger player. Disguised sales tend to be short-lived, rarely lasting more than five years.

Bootstrap Alliances

A strong company and a weak one often form this type of partnership, but it rarely works. The weak company attempts to use the alliance to improve its capabilities. Usually the weak partner remains weak and is acquired by the stronger partner. In the few cases where this strategy is successful, the partnership develops into an alliance of equals or the partners separate after the weak partner has achieved the ability to compete on its own.

Evolutions to a Sale

These alliances start with two strong and compatible partners, but competitive tensions develop, bargaining power shifts, and one of the partners ultimately sells out to the other. However, these alliances often succeed in meeting the initial objectives of the partners and may exceed the seven-year average life span for alliances.

Alliances of Complementary Equals

This type of alliance involves two strong and complementary partners that remain strong during the course of the alliance. These mutually beneficial relationships are likely to last much longer than seven years.

Notes

1. Yves Doz and Gary Hamel, "The Use of Alliances in Implementing Technology Strategies," in *Managing Technology and Innovation for Corporate Renewal,* ed. Yves Doz (Oxford: Oxford University Press).

Originally published in January–February 1995
Reprint 95102

Use Joint Ventures to Ease the Pain of Restructuring

ASHISH NANDA AND PETER J. WILLIAMSON

Executive Summary

THE PROVERBIAL "DOGS" have been closed, and high-performing noncore businesses have gone to the highest bidders. For large corporations that are refocusing their portfolios, the problem of how best to dispose of basically sound but underperforming businesses remains. Putting a business up for sale can be its kiss of death, with employee morale plummeting and prospective buyers unaware of the business's true potential value.

The solution may be a restructuring joint venture, an arrangement that allows the buyer to learn about the business's untapped possibilities before buying it outright, and that often results in higher returns to the seller than a straight sale would. The authors contrast the successful joint venture involving Whirlpool and Philips with the disastrous results of Maytag's purchase of Chicago Pacific Corporation.

47

Restructuring joint ventures work especially well for businesses whose assets are intangible and therefore hard for a potential buyer to gauge. In the case of IBM's Rolm Systems Division and Siemens of Germany, for instance, IBM sold outright that portion of the Rolm business in which the primary assets were tangible and transferred the rest to Siemens through a joint venture. As this example also shows, buyers often use the joint venture as an opportunity to enter new markets beyond their national borders.

The management burden imposed by restructuring joint ventures can be heavy, and the partners must plan carefully for the end of the alliance to avoid value-destroying conflicts. However, the benefits of these ventures can more than make up for the effort required.

THE PROVERBIAL "DOGS" have been closed. Businesses with marketable assets such as real estate or modern plants have been sold off. High-performing noncore businesses have gone to the highest bidders. For large corporations intent on refocusing their portfolios, a seemingly intractable problem remains: how best to dispose of basically sound but underperforming businesses that do not fit the corporation's vision. Lacking high-quality physical assets and suffering from a chronic lack of corporate attention, noncore businesses may nevertheless have formidable brands, enviable distribution power, skilled and experienced people, and proprietary systems. Competitors would take years to develop the same intangible assets. Restructuring CEOs appreciate these sources of value, but because the businesses are not central to the corporate portfolio, the investments of time and money necessary to develop them into world-class operations cannot be justified.

When seeking to sell businesses such as these, the restructuring CEO faces two fundamental issues. One is how to convey what the business is really worth to a potential purchaser: to make the unknown known. The potential buyers' natural reaction is to discount what cannot be assessed. They will not pay a premium for what they cannot see, touch, or measure. Buyers also may wonder, What weaknesses of the business do the sellers know about that we don't? Why are they selling, anyway? As a result, when the main value of the business lies in intangibles, the bids that arrive are substantially below what the restructurer believes is fair.

Labeling a business "for sale" causes a blanket of uncertainty to descend on everyone.

The second issue is how to maintain the health of the business during the process of selling it. Put another way, how can the corporation maintain the commitment of all the stakeholders during the disposal phase? Labeling a business "for sale" may result in distracted employees and distrustful customers, distributors, and vendors. Hence, putting a business up for auction is more likely to reduce its value than enhance it. With the corporation unable to resolve these issues, the business is left in limbo. The corporation cannot muster the investment required to restore the business's competitiveness, yet it is unwilling to endure the pain of putting the business up for sale, knowing that it will net only a fraction of its true worth.

Joint ventures, traditionally pursued only as a means to expand into new businesses, offer a way out of this restructuring impasse. Companies such as Philips,

Corning, Dresser, IBM, and Honeywell have used joint ventures creatively to exit from noncore businesses. (See the exhibit "Pioneers in the Use of Joint Ventures for Restructuring.") In so doing, these pioneers have departed from convention in the design and management of their joint ventures. Although some of the rules of thumb for joint ventures still apply, other ideas must be turned on their heads.

The Joint Venture as a Restructuring Tool: The Philips-Whirlpool Case

Take the example of Philips, the Dutch electronics multinational. When Philips sought to reorganize its diverse portfolio in the late 1980s, it identified the $1.55 billion major domestic appliances division as not essential to its future. The division was supporting nine different brands. Sales and distribution were not coordinated across either countries or brands, resulting in inefficiencies and overlaps. Production was spread haphazardly across ten plants in five countries—plants that were desperately in need of huge capital injections if they were ever to develop into world-class facilities. Running these operations was an army of 14,000 employees, many protected by European legislation on job security. Given its history of poor performance, an outright sale of the division would have fetched Philips only a fire-sale price.

Despite these problems, Philips management knew that the appliances division had potentially valuable assets, including pockets of underutilized manufacturing skills, some of Europe's best-known brands, world-class design expertise, and a pan-European distribution network that placed it number two behind Electrolux in European market share. Unfortunately, those strengths

Pioneers in the Use of Joint Ventures for Restructuring

Restructurer (A)	Incoming Partner (B)	Business	JV Start	Partner's Shares (A–B)	JV Termination	Outcome
Philips	Whirlpool	consumer appliances	1989	47–53	1991	Philips received a substantially higher price than it would have through direct sale. Whirlpool established a strong European presence.
Corning	Ciba-Geigy	medical diagnostics	1985	50–50	1989	Ciba-Geigy entered the U.S. market as a major player. Corning rid itself of a peripheral business without destroying the business's value.
Honeywell	Bull & NEC	mainframe computers	1987	42.5–42.5–15	1991	Honeywell exited the mainframe-computer business and refocused on its electronic control business. Bull established a substantial presence outside France. NEC developed a channel for marketing its computers in the United States.
Dresser	Komatsu	construction equipment	1988	50–50	1994	Dresser disposed of its noncore construction equipment business. Komatsu strengthened its U.S. presence.
IBM	Siemens	marketing, distribution, and service of PBX systems	1989	50–50	1992	IBM exited the price-competitive supplementary business. Siemens strengthened its presence in the U.S. telecommunications market.

were undercut by the division's inability to achieve global scale in the design, procurement, and production of components. Identified as noncore, the appliances division was usually last in line for scarce management attention and corporate cash.

Whirlpool Corporation was the obvious buyer. Whirlpool management was looking to expand beyond its U.S. base. It appreciated the benefits of inheriting a major European position in an industry that was rapidly becoming global. Whirlpool sensed that it could radically alter the cost structure of the business if it sourced components globally, coordinated production, sales, and distribution across countries and product lines, and rationalized production. If it took over the business, Whirlpool would invest in new plants and machinery and transfer its own advanced manufacturing processes to the European operations.

However, Whirlpool's executives were less convinced than Philips's about the potential of the business. How strong was the consumer franchise behind the nine brands? Would the network of dealers remain loyal in the face of massive change? How much time and money would it take to transform the unmotivated federation of businesses into a lean and focused operation? Both parties ran the numbers, but their widely different assumptions and market experiences produced valuations that were not even close. A strategically sensible deal was foundering on the issue of price.

A joint venture proved to be the solution. In 1989, Philips offered Whirlpool 53% of its appliances business for $381 million along with an option to buy the remaining 47% within three years. Whirlpool found the arrangement very attractive: It provided the company with an opportunity to learn about the reality of the appliances division as an insider and to initiate improvement plans before taking over the division entirely. For Philips, the joint venture provided the opportunity to prove to Whirlpool that the business really was as valuable as it claimed.

Whirlpool moved fast to breathe new life into the business. It quickly imported technology from its other operations abroad, developed common platforms, and standardized components across factories, reducing inventory by more than a third. It identified common suppliers across countries, and cut the total number of suppliers in half. Pan-European advertising campaigns were initiated, and sales operations were integrated across Europe. Furthermore, the joint venture retained the appliances division's best talent, employees remained motivated, and customers and dealers stayed loyal. The joint venture transformed the business into a vibrant and profitable operation.

Whirlpool benefited also from Philips's continued involvement in the business. Philips management acted as a sounding board for Whirlpool's marketing decisions. Philips shared its support systems with Whirlpool, especially its IT facilities, to give Whirlpool time to get its own support systems up and running. For a period of time, Whirlpool's products were double branded as Philips-Whirlpool appliances, allowing Whirlpool the luxury of using the Philips brand name so well recognized throughout Europe while gradually introducing its own brand name.

Whirlpool exercised its option in 1991, purchasing the remaining 47% share for $610 million, and Philips exited the business smoothly and on substantially more favorable terms—the uplift was estimated at $270 million—than if it had simply put the business on the auction block in 1989.

Unlocking Imprisoned Assets

As the success of the Philips-Whirlpool alliance demonstrates, forming a joint venture to sell an underperforming but high-potential business has several advantages over a conventional sale:

STAKEHOLDERS STAY ENGAGED AND COMMITTED

The announcement that a division is for sale can be its kiss of death. A blanket of uncertainty descends on everyone. Improvement plans are put on ice and high-caliber people leave for other opportunities. Those who remain divert their energies into polishing up their résumés and renewing their contacts with placement agencies. Customers and distributors fret about the continuity of after-sales service and technical support, the limited possibility of future product enhancements, and the danger of being saddled with obsolete inventory. Vendors suspect that their relationship is likely to end, so they tighten their credit terms and relax their delivery and service standards. Investors, concerned that the business must be in bad shape to have been put up for sale, unload their shares. A spiral of retrenchment, plummeting performance, and declining stock-market value often results.

Ciba Corning shows how a joint venture can be used to maintain continuity and commitment as ownership is transferred from one company to the other. In 1985,

Corning was trying to exit the U.S. medical diagnostics business. Ciba-Geigy, a Swiss pharmaceuticals giant, was seeking to enter the U.S. market. The two companies agreed to convert Corning's medical diagnostics business into a fifty-fifty joint venture—Ciba Corning—against a payment of $75 million from Ciba-Geigy to Corning. During the three years in which the business operated as a joint venture, employees, customers, and vendors stayed loyal to the enterprise, confident that Ciba-Geigy was committed to strengthening Ciba Corning and was investing in its long-term future. Ciba-Geigy integrated the business into its global operations, and Corning demonstrated the intrinsic quality of its medical diagnostics division to Ciba. In 1989, Ciba-Geigy bought out Corning's remaining 50% share in the venture for $150 million. Upon the termination of the joint venture, Richard Dulude, group president at Corning, remarked, "I think both of the partners would say that [it] was a successful relationship. It allowed us both to do things we wanted to do; it strengthened [Ciba Corning] significantly. It ended up in the Ciba-Geigy fold, and it will be much stronger because of that."[1] The business created an estimated $75 million of value partly because disruptions such as employee turnover and desertions of suppliers and distributors were minimized.

This is not to say that a restructuring joint venture guarantees that all employees will be retained. Any restructuring process is likely to involve plant closings and layoffs, and the restructuring joint venture is no exception. In the Philips-Whirlpool joint venture, for instance, Whirlpool management closed a plant in Barcelona and trimmed the workforce by more than 2,000 people as part of its restructuring program. Even so, the motivational benefit remains: A restructuring joint venture signals that the business will be invested in rather than allowed to deteriorate slowly or shut down completely. This process of change and improvement may demand sacrifices initially, but everyone knows that the goal is to restore the competitiveness of the business.

Participating in a joint venture reduces the risk that the buyer will land an expensive lemon or make an uninformed decision.

Also, joint ventures allow employees to make a considered choice: Stay with the business under its new management or migrate back to the restructurer.

THE UNKNOWN BECOMES KNOWN

A joint venture allows the buyer to gain an understanding of the business that is inaccessible to an outsider, even one who engages in the most thorough of due diligence. The buyer is able to assess the true value of such intangible assets as brands, distribution networks, people, and systems and to understand through direct involvement over an extended period how the business operates. This experience reduces the risk that the buyer will land an expensive lemon or make an uninformed decision. In the Philips-Whirlpool joint venture, Whirlpool was able to observe pockets of marketing excellence and to achieve a deep understanding of European distribution channels. This allowed it to make key decisions quickly and effectively on brand strengthening, plant closure, and supplier rationalization well before it assumed complete ownership of the business. Of course, those benefits came at a price: The eventual purchase price reflected the reduction in risk. Philips's final exit price from its major appliances business showed a significant premium over Whirlpool's initial offer.

In contrast to the approach that Whirlpool took, when Maytag Corporation wanted to enter the European white-goods market in 1989, it chose to do so by buying Chicago Pacific Corporation, which owned the Hoover appliances line. Maytag is a venerable 86-year-old Iowa-based appliances manufacturer known for its cautious management and homespun values. Because it had used acquisition rather than joint venturing as its entry vehicle, Maytag management had no opportunity to observe operations as an insider and thereby come to understand the business before taking on total responsibility for running it. The new management, dispatched by Maytag as a special task force, was charged with bringing about "rebirth and rejuvenation" at Hoover. Coming from the United States, where distribution remained relatively fragmented, the management team may have thought it obvious that it should build on Hoover's traditionally strong relationships with small retailers. But, as former Hoover executives later remarked, the new team did not realize how different selling and distribution had become in the 1990s in Britain, where six major retailers with substantial bargaining power now dominated the market.

The lack of a transition period during which the new management team could acquire a thorough understanding of the British market proved costly. Problems reached a head in 1993 when the new team ran a promotional campaign in Great Britain and Ireland offering free airplane tickets with major appliance purchases. Such a promotion probably wouldn't have created a stir in the United States, where promotional giveaways are common and discounted airplane tickets are widely available. In contrast, giveaways are a rarity in Europe and airfares remain regulated and expensive. Consumers were excited by the golden opportunity to enjoy flights they couldn't otherwise afford. Hoover management was shocked when, contrary to its expectations, more than 220,000 customers (roughly one of every 300 people in Britain and Ireland) flocked to buy the appliances, many of them simply to receive the free flights. The cost of the promotion soon exceeded the contribution it was bringing in. Hoover had to take a $50 million charge to honor the commitments of its promotion, even as it began facing stiff competition from an active market in secondhand Hoover appliances. Leonard Hadley, Maytag's CEO, remarked that the fiasco left the impression that those in charge were "a group of bumbling fools."[2] The imbroglio led to the firing of Hoover's president and two senior marketing executives. Eventually, unhappy with how the business was performing, Maytag disposed of the European portion of the Hoover appliances line in June of this year, booking a $130 million loss in the process.

THE BUYER RECEIVES CONTINUED MANAGERIAL AND TECHNICAL INPUT FROM THE RESTRUCTURER

Outright purchase generally means that a business's connection with its corporate parent is cut abruptly, and the separation can wound both the business being divested and other businesses that may be enmeshed with it. A joint venture, by contrast, allows continuity of access to the former parent's assets, brand equity, systems, and services. Continued support from the restructurer—in the form of knowledge, technology, and skills—is invaluable during the difficult process of rejuvenating and streamlining the business. The restructurer wants to earn as high an exit price as possible, and that price is determined by the success of the joint venture. This means that the restructurer has every motivation to tutor the buying partner in running the business. Recall how Whirlpool relied on Philips to provide the appliances division with IT services and brand support early in the life of the joint venture.

Executives must ask two questions: What is the nature of the restructuring problem and what really are the buyer's goals?

Contrast this with an outright sale, in which the new owner is handed a hot potato with little guidance on how to manage the business. Before the sale is consummated, the seller may be reluctant to give away too much information on running the business for fear that the buyer will not pay for the value it gets from the information: The buyer may take the information and never close the deal. And after a sale, the seller has little incentive to hold the hand of a nervous buyer. So the new owner is forced to learn how to manage the business both on the run and in the dark. A joint venture ensures that a knowledgeable tutor is on hand to guide the newcomer through a minefield of decisions in which a misstep could very well destroy the value of the business being transferred. In the Ciba Corning joint venture, for instance, Corning's staff was actively involved in the business, interacting intensively with Ciba-Geigy's corporate team during the life of the joint venture. Corning's input was especially valuable in introducing Ciba-Geigy to Corning's loyal distributors and customers and in providing Ciba-Geigy management with a good understanding of the market and competition in the U.S. medical diagnostics industry.

Deciding When a Joint Venture Makes Sense

In making a hard-nosed assessment of whether a joint venture will indeed be an effective sales vehicle, executives should address two key questions: What precisely is the nature of our restructuring problem and what really are the buyer's goals?

THE NATURE OF THE RESTRUCTURING PROBLEM

Joint ventures are most effective when the task of disentangling a business from the systems and structures of its corporate parent is likely to be slow and complex. This is often the case when a company has to unwind a related diversification or a vertical integration. In cases where several businesses share facilities, systems, personnel, or administrative backup, joint venturing provides the grace period for a smooth and gradual separation. The arguments in favor of using a joint venture are less compelling if the business being sold is an entirely freestanding unit. When General Motors wished to exit from the information technology services business, outright sale made sense, because it would not be difficult to separate the EDS subsidiary from GM's automobile interests.

Consider, on the other hand, Dresser Industries, a diversified conglomerate with 1985 sales in excess of $4 billion. When Dresser embarked on a strategy of sharpening its focus, it faced a major challenge in disposing of its construction equipment subsidiary. This billion-dollar business had a widely recognized brand name and a strong distribution network in the construction equipment business, but Dresser did not consider it to be a core business and had neglected it. The construction equipment business shared its marketing, distribution, and facilities with other earthmoving businesses in Dresser's portfolio. Its 3.5 million square feet of factory space were spread over eight factories in the United States, Canada, and Brazil. If Dresser had chosen to cut the construction equipment business out for immediate disposal, untidy threads would have been left hanging.

Japan's Komatsu was a potential buyer. Komatsu was committed to the construction equipment industry: It was number two globally and it spent ten times more than Dresser's subsidiary on research and development. Komatsu wanted to strengthen its presence in the United States in order to compete more effectively on global leader Caterpillar's home turf. However, a direct purchase of Dresser's operations was not very attractive. Komatsu would have had to put up with the delays and disruptions associated with the untangling of Dresser's construction equipment business from the other parts of the company.

In 1988, the two companies found a way out of this predicament by converting the construction equipment business into Komatsu Dresser Company, a fifty-fifty joint venture. The KDC partnership helped Komatsu use Dresser's manufacturing facilities and network of dealers in the United States. Dresser's construction equipment business gained access to Komatsu's total quality systems and lean-manufacturing know-how—essential ingredients for restoring the construction equipment business's quality standards and for improving its efficiency. As part of the joint venture agreement, Komatsu and Dresser each invested an initial $75 million to upgrade the factories by introducing robots and flexible machining centers. The joint venture also offered Dresser the luxury of slowly but surely disentangling the distribution network and the facilities of its earthmoving business from its other operations. Eventually, in 1992, four years after the joint venture had been established, Dresser spun off its ownership in the joint venture into a separate company, Indresco. John Murphy, Dresser's chairman, remarked on the occasion, "This is the culmination of a program that has been underway for several years. . . . [It] will enable Dresser to devote all of its available resources to its core energy-related operations and at the same time will provide greater growth opportunities for the unrelated business segments."[3]

A joint venture is of much more value to a buyer that plans to apply its own assets and skills to nurturing the business.

The joint venture solution also is better than immediate sale when the most important assets in the business being sold are intangibles—a consumer franchise, distribution relationships, human resources, perhaps systems. Consider the restructuring of IBM's troubled Rolm Systems Division in partnership with Siemens of Germany. IBM wanted to exit the thin-margin, price-competitive PBX market and Siemens wanted to strengthen its presence in U.S. telecommunications. For those parts of the Rolm business in which the primary assets were tangible, as in manufacturing, the parties chose a straightforward sale from IBM to Siemens. For those activities relating to the customer, in which most of the potential value was locked up in intangibles, transfer through a joint venture was the preferred solution. So, in a concurrent deal, IBM and Siemens formed a fifty-fifty joint venture to handle marketing, distribution, and service for the Rolm product line. Entering into a joint venture ensured continuity for the dealers and the customers, and also helped Siemens gauge the worth of Rolm's brand franchise and customer relationships before it had to pay for the entire business. In 1992, three years after the joint venture was set up, IBM exited, leaving Rolm entirely in Siemens's fold. Of the 4,500 joint venture employees, only about 50 transferred back to IBM; the rest stayed on as Siemens employees. During the course of the joint venture, Siemens had paid IBM an estimated $1.1 billion to purchase Rolm. Analysts considered this amount handsome compensation for a loss-making and troubled business. On the other hand, they also commented that Siemens had minimized the potential downside of entering the U.S. telecommunications market.

THE GOALS OF THE BUYING PARTNER

Asset strippers who want to shut down most of the acquisition's operations and transfer only the customers or the brands to their own products will not be interested in a deal that involves the complexity, subtlety, cost, and attention that a joint venture is likely to require. A joint venture is of much more relevance—and value—to a potential buyer that plans to apply its own assets and skills to nurturing the business as it learns about it. Consider the case of Honeywell and Compagnie des Machines Bull (Groupe Bull). Although Honeywell was a $2 billion business, it was barely profitable, and its share of the U.S. mainframe computer market had fallen to 2.4% by 1986. Honeywell management wanted to exit the computer business and focus on its global electronic controls operations. Some potential buyers could have viewed Honeywell's computer business as a bundle of tangible salable assets—real estate and equipment—and an installed customer base that could be converted to the acquirer's systems. But Bull had different objectives. It wanted to develop a global presence beyond its predominantly French base and intended to build any business it acquired overseas as an ongoing concern. In 1987, Honeywell's computer operations were converted into a joint venture in which Honeywell and Groupe Bull each took a 42.5% share. A third partner, Japan's NEC Corporation, took a 15% share because it saw the joint venture as a good way to help sell its high-performance computers in the European and U.S. markets.

Groupe Bull and NEC participated in several rounds of recapitalization, increasing Bull's joint venture share in the process while Honeywell's share gradually declined. The cash infusions were used to double capital outlays, cut time to market by three-fourths, step up research and development expenditure, initiate an extensive advertising campaign, and enter the U.S. personal computers market by acquiring Zenith Electronics' computer business. Finally, in 1991, Honeywell sold off its remaining share in the business to Bull, leaving Bull and NEC with 85% and 15% stakes in the business, respectively.

Minimizing the Burden on Management

Given the benefits of joint venturing, why do many companies still choose to sell their businesses? And when they do choose to enter into a joint venture, why don't they maintain the partnership on an ongoing basis? A key reason is that joint venturing requires more of management's time and attention than does single ownership. This is what we call the management burden of joint venturing. Joint venture managers find that satisfying several corporate masters is arduous and time consuming. Richard Dulude of Corning went so far as to say that a wholly owned subsidiary takes twice as much effort to manage as a joint venture takes. Communications must often be duplicated, and contradictory signals from the two parents have to be resolved. Plans to minimize this burden must be put in place before joint venturing can provide an effective way to dispose of a business.

To minimize the management burden without reducing the effectiveness of the joint venture, executives need to focus on three central tasks: ensuring goal alignment, bridging the cultural divide, and selecting staff who can manage effectively without an elaborate organizational framework.

For any joint venture to operate smoothly, it is absolutely critical that the partners share a commonality of purpose. This holds true for restructuring joint ventures as well. But given that restructuring joint ventures must evolve flexibly as ownership and management responsibility is transferred from one party to the other, a straitjacket of legal documentation designed to force the partners together won't work. Instead, the partners' goals must be brought in line by developing and maintaining the right informal links, starting at the top of both organizations. James Houghton, Corning's CEO, has described the kind of relationship that is required: "We have grown up in this company with the Dow Corning success, where a handshake sealed an agreement [in 1943] and led to a

remarkable partnership. . . . [Even today,] I make a
point of getting together with the top person from each of
our major partners once or twice a year, just to have
lunch, and look the person in the eye to make sure our
strategic visions match."[4]

Although critical to the success of a restructuring
joint venture, the commitment of top management is
not enough. Of equal importance is the need to identify
and resolve, right at the beginning of the joint venture,
the cultural differences between the lower-level executives of the parties coming together. In the case of
Dresser and Komatsu, the cultural differences that
emerged between the executives of the two companies
soon led to animosity. Former Dresser executives complained that managers from Komatsu were making crucial decisions during Friday evening bull sessions conducted in Japanese. Executives from Komatsu felt that
former Dresser executives were interacting with them in
a spirit of competitiveness, not cooperation. Rivalries
among the executives spilled over into bickering between
the Komatsu and Dresser dealers.

Those dissensions had a severe impact on performance. KDC's sales fell from $1.36 billion in 1989 to $940
million in 1991, its U.S. market share fell from 20% to
18%, and the company was awash in red ink. Belated
tackling of these problems demanded a phenomenal
amount of attention from management. Distribution
lines were consolidated, plants were shut down, and the
workforce was slashed from 5,000 in 1988 to only 3,000 in
1992. Senior executives hurriedly put together crash
courses in cross-cultural sensitivity training and pulled
their remaining subordinates from routine activities to
attend these programs. Foresight and systematic planning to close the cultural gap between the two partners

could have minimized the disruption and pain that the joint venture was forced to experience.

The third key to reducing the management burden is to ensure that the joint venture runs with minimal structure. Putting too much formal structure in place creates problems: It adds to overhead and it complicates the task of unwinding the joint venture when the time comes for a buyout to be consummated. The way to remain lean and yet effective is to staff the joint venture with people who are comfortable exercising responsibility despite lacking complete authority, and who have the capability to nurture relationships across organizational, geographic, and cultural boundaries. As one Corning executive explains, managers who "rely less on formal power and share more information" flourish in this sort of joint venture. Companies hoping to restructure through joint ventures should carefully audit their personnel to ensure that they do have the requisite skills to manage the joint ventures effectively. The restructurer may have to make some tough decisions, such as choosing a person with strong interpersonal skills even if others are more technically competent. Before committing to the joint venture, each partner should also carefully consider the interpersonal qualities of the managers the other partner is going to assign to it. The partners should use that information to evaluate how much attention the joint venture will demand once it is set up.

Negotiating the Deal: Attention to the Beginning and the End

In a typical growth-oriented joint venture, few deal makers would recommend as a centerpiece of negotiations an analysis of why the business has been performing badly. Fewer still might suggest that a plan to terminate the joint venture form the core of the contract. Conventional wisdom would caution against ceding too much management control. It also would frown at the idea that a joint venture should be built on loose ties rather than on a tightly defined infrastructure. But those are exactly the design ingredients likely to promote a successful restructuring joint venture.

ACKNOWLEDGING THE BUSINESS'S UNDERPERFORMANCE AND ESTIMATING ITS POTENTIAL

When negotiating the transfer of an existing business into a joint venture, the restructurer needs to inform the prospective partner about the causes of the business's underperformance. At first pass, this focus on the negatives may seem paradoxical. But remember, the buyer's primary interest is in the upside potential. The restructurer should emphasize the gap between the business's current performance and what it could achieve in the right hands. In converting their businesses to joint ventures, neither Philips nor Dresser glossed over the poor performance of their businesses; they highlighted to their potential partners the improvements that could be implemented if existing operations were combined with the incoming partners' assets and capabilities.

From the buyer's perspective, a restructurer's willingness to enter a joint venture is a good omen, a signal of the restructurer's confidence in the business's potential. In fact, a buyer should view very skeptically any claims of hidden potential if a restructurer is prepared to sell the business only in a one-shot deal. Recall that Whirlpool's initial valuation of the Philips appliances business was considerably below Philips's own estimate. But when Philips offered to back the business in a transitory joint venture, Whirlpool was reassured that the business possessed valuable intangible assets, and a deal was struck.

SHARING FINANCIAL STAKES WHILE SHIFTING MANAGEMENT CONTROL

When joint ventures are designed to build a new business, both parties often vie for the majority share and clear management control. In a restructuring joint venture, however, it is frequently to the restructurer's advantage to share ownership equally with the buying partner and yet to cede management control from day one. Equal—or near equal—financial stakes ensure joint commitment, but giving the buying partner management control allows that partner to bring its own capabilities and skills to bear on the business quickly and efficiently. The successful joint ventures that we have observed— Philips-Whirlpool, Ciba Corning, and IBM-Siemens— had both partners taking roughly equal stakes in the business with the incoming partner swiftly taking charge.

The initial ownership share the buying partner seeks in the joint venture signals the partner's long-term intentions to the restructurer. Potential buyers who are looking for a substantial financial share in the joint venture will want to take charge of the business immediately. In such an instance, the restructurer should expect the joint venture to be of short duration and should be prepared to demonstrate to the buyer the true potential of the business very early in the partnership. On the other hand, a buying partner taking too small a share and treating the joint venture simply as a speculative low-cost play among its options can create significant problems for the restructurer.

Consider the unraveling of the recent Honda-Rover joint venture. From 1979 to 1988, Honda Motor Company supported the troubled British car manufacturer through a combination of licensing, supply arrangements, and joint development. In 1988, British Aerospace bought Rover, and in 1990 it engaged in a share swap in which Honda U.K. and Rover each acquired 20% of the other's equity. By 1993, British Aerospace had decided to focus on its core aerospace and defense activities and to exit the car business, so it approached Honda offering to let Honda raise its share in Rover to 47.5%, with the possibility of full ownership at a later date. Honda was not interested in raising its shareholding in Rover at the price or the pace that British Aerospace wanted, so British Aerospace then turned around and sold its share to BMW. Honda and Rover untangled their cross-shareholdings over the next several months amid bitter acrimony.

PLANNING FOR THE TERMINATION OF THE VENTURE

For most companies entering a traditional joint venture, writing a termination clause is as unthinkable as writing a divorce clause would be for a couple entering matrimony. But remember that a restructuring joint venture is actually a phased sale and is meant to be transitory. Success in a joint venture that is transitory by design is measured not by the longevity of the alliance but by the smoothness with which ownership of the business is transferred and by the value that is created. Termination is a natural step in the evolution of a restructuring joint venture, and it makes sense to plan ahead of time for an orderly disentanglement. Otherwise, value-destroying conflicts can arise between the partners. One partner may seek dissolution of the alliance while the other wants to continue it. Remember that both the Philips-Whirlpool and the Honeywell-Bull-NEC alliances included timebound buyout clauses.

To convey their confidence in the potential of the business, restructurers often leave the trigger for terminating the joint venture entirely in the hands of the potential buyer. The restructurer may offer the buyer an option to purchase the rest of the business within a specified time window. Recall that Honeywell's joint venture with Groupe Bull had both parties taking a 42.5% stake, while Japan's NEC purchased the remaining 15% share. As part of the original agreement, Bull had the option to buy a further 27% of shares from Honeywell after one year. Subsequent recapitalizations of the joint venture culminated in Honeywell's exiting the business completely. The option, but not the requirement, for Bull to raise its stake conveyed Honeywell's confidence in the business as well as its willingness to contribute and remain involved with the business in order to help Bull build it up. Honeywell's graduated exit also provided Bull with a manageable period in which it could gradually take control of the business.

If the buyer is given an option to purchase, the purchase price of the remaining shares can be made contingent on how the buyer enjoys the taste of the business. When Siemens bought into Rolm in 1989, it agreed to pay IBM between $850 million and $1.2 billion, depending on future profits. The total payment Siemens ended up making when it finally bought all of Rolm was closer to the higher figure at $1.1 billion. Making the final purchase price contingent on performance implies that the buyer does not have to pay a high price if the business continues to perform poorly even after restructuring. When Komatsu bought the remaining 50% share in the troubled KDC joint venture from Indresco, the Dresser spinoff, all it had to pay in consideration was $60 million—the approximate pro rata book value of the shares—in addition to assuming $180 million of contingent debt liability.

However, like most types of insurance, this protection doesn't come free. Making price dependent on performance means that if the business performs significantly above expectations, the buyer must make a much larger payment for the remaining shares. Such a contract also gives the restructurer a powerful incentive to help ensure that prospective synergies with the buyer's capabilities are indeed achieved. In the examples we have cited above, the buyers judged the benefits of such deals to be worth the hefty premiums they have had to pay. Both Corning and Philips, for instance, netted much more at the termination than they did at the beginning of their joint ventures with Ciba-Geigy and Whirlpool respectively.

Faced with today's restructuring challenges, CEOs need to look at the role of joint ventures in a new light. Pioneering companies have shown that joint venturing is a powerful tool for unlocking imprisoned assets within a corporate portfolio. A joint venture provides a way for a restructurer to exit a business smoothly and puts more cash into shareholders' pockets than would an outright sale. For the buyer, a joint venture reduces the risk of ending up with a lemon. It ensures that the business is transferred in good shape without the damage and disruption so often associated with a straight sale, which forces the business first to land and then to take off with an inexperienced crew. The joint venture solution is more like the handover between relief crews in flight. Of course, restructuring partnerships must be handled differently from the way conventional joint ventures are handled, but the benefits to be had more than make up for the effort required, and will no doubt lead to an increase in their use in the future.

Notes

1. "Corning: Joint Ventures as a Key to Global Growth," *M&A Europe*, September–October 1990, p. 48.

2. Gregory E. David, "Breaking the Spell," *Financial World*, May 10, 1994, p. 36.

3. "Dresser Industries Makes Announcement," *Southwest Newswire*, February 5, 1992.

4. "Corning Inc.: A Network of Alliances," HBS case no. 391–102, August 12, 1992.

Originally published in November–December 1995
Reprint 95608

Group Versus Group

How Alliance Networks Compete

BENJAMIN GOMES-CASSERES

Executive Summary

COLLABORATION IN BUSINESS is no longer confined
to conventional two-company alliances, such as joint ventures or marketing accords. Today groups of companies
are linking together for a common purpose. Consequently, a new form of competition is spreading across
global markets: group versus group. Call them networks,
clusters, constellations, or virtual corporations, these
groups consist of companies joined together in a larger
overarching relationship. The individual companies in
any group differ in size and focus, but they fulfill specific
roles within their group. Furthermore, within the network
or group, companies may be linked to one another
through various kinds of alliances, ranging from the formality of an equity joint venture to the informality of a
loose collaboration.

Are alliance groups the wave of the future or a passing fad. Have they actually helped group members compete more effectively?

Too little empirical evidence exists to answer these questions with assurance. But we do know enough, based on the experiences of the pioneers in group-based competition, such as Mips Computer Systems, to examine the questions that senior executives should be asking themselves before they organize, dive into, or decide to forgo these multi-alliance networks. Networks offer obvious advantages to their members, but those advantages come with costs that are not so obvious.

COLLABORATION IN BUSINESS is no longer confined to conventional two-company alliances, such as joint ventures or marketing accords. Today we see groups of companies linking themselves together for a common purpose. Consequently, a new form of competition is spreading across global markets: group versus group.

Call them networks, clusters, constellations, or virtual corporations, these groups consist of companies joined together in a larger, overarching relationship. The individual companies in any group differ in size and focus, but they fulfill specific roles within their group. Furthermore, within the network or group, companies may be linked to one another through various kinds of alliances, ranging from the formality of an equity joint venture to the informality of a loose collaboration.

A prime example of such an alliance group was built between 1987 and 1991 by Silicon Valley start-up Mips Computer Systems, which has since been acquired by Silicon Graphics. Mips developed a huge network of alliances to promote its new microprocessor technology. And networks exist in other industries, too, where they are often created to maximize joint volume in order to exploit economies of scale. For example, Swissair's alliances with Delta Air Lines, Singapore Airlines, and SAS sought to increase bookings on transatlantic and European-Asian flights and to combine the procurement and maintenance of airplanes. In automobiles, General Motors' network of partners, which includes Toyota, Isuzu, Suzuki, and Saab, competes globally with a group of Ford partners, consisting of Nissan, Mazda, Kia, and Jaguar. In the multimedia field, an array of alliance groups has sprung up in the past two years as the computer and communications industries have converged. Computer companies have joined with consumer electronics companies, cable TV operators, telecommunications providers, and entertainment companies to develop new products and services.

Are alliance groups the wave of the future or a passing fad? Have they actually helped group members compete more effectively?

Too little empirical evidence exists as yet to answer these questions with complete assurance. But we do know enough, based on the experiences of the pioneers in group-based competition, to examine the questions that senior executives should be asking themselves before they organize, dive into, or decide to forgo these alliance networks. Networks offer obvious advantages to their members. However, those advantages come with costs that may not be so obvious.

The Growth of Group-Based Competition

How did this idea of networks of alliances arise? For one, there is the influence of the global economy. In the 1950s and 1960s, companies based in the United States were for the most part unchallenged in their technology, marketing skills, and ability to manage large-scale businesses. In the global environment of the 1980s and 1990s, however, companies all over the world have matched or approximated the achievements of those U.S.-based companies. The change is dramatic in industries like computers, where newcomers can ride the wave of new technologies, and in mature industries like automobiles, where new entrants can adapt more readily to changing market demands. As a result, it's essential for U.S. companies to develop relationships with peers abroad—if only to remain abreast of important external developments and perhaps to influence them.

Another recent factor favoring the formation of alliance groups is the growing complexity of products and services, and of their design, production, and delivery. It's the rare product today that doesn't contain components incorporating wholly distinct and specialized technologies. It's the rare service today whose performance doesn't combine several specialized skills. And it's the rare business today that doesn't rely for its raw materials, marketing, or distribution on people with diverse technological or market-specific skills. Finding and assembling all those assets under a single roof is difficult, to say the least. Often, it's not even desirable. Because the greatest advantages of specialization and of scale are often realized at the component rather than at the system level, companies may do best to focus on the component level while forming ties to one another in order to manage system-level interdependence.

Networks are giving companies access to skills in different countries.

In response to these changes in the competitive environment, companies have created networks of alliances in order to command competitive advantages that individual companies or traditional two-company alliances cannot. Networks have distinct advantages in three kinds of situations in particular.

First, network competition is growing in battles over technical standards. In emerging industries, various technologies may contend for market share. The outcome of this battle often depends on the number of companies adopting each technology. Alliance networks can help contending companies promote their technologies and gain the critical mass required to persuade more businesses to use their design. To do that, they must persuade enough "sponsors" to join their group. They also count on a snowball effect to help them: the more machines they sell incorporating their technology, the more software will be written for that technology, which in turn will help sell more machines, and so on.

Second, the increasing importance of global scale has created a fertile ground for alliance networks. Linking with local companies in various markets may help a company spread its costs over larger volumes or give it access to skills and assets in different nations. While networks of wholly owned subsidiaries can also be used, regulatory barriers or the need for rapid expansion sometimes preclude this option. Consider alliance groups in the airline industry. Deregulation in the United States, the rise of the hub-and-spoke system, and the economic integration of Europe increased the value of scale and scope in the industry during the 1980s and 1990s. Only those companies able to spread their operations over multiple national markets earn a profit. In addition, airlines with large domestic feeder networks can expect higher load factors on long intercontinental flights. Smaller carriers, such as Swissair, had no choice but to link up with other airlines.

Third, new technologies are creating links between industries that were formerly separate. Networks allow specialists in each field to cooperate and exploit new opportunities much faster than if each were to try to acquire the industry-specific skills and assets of the others. For example, consider the networks of alliances emerging in the multimedia field, where computer technology is merging with telecommunications, video, and audio technologies. Several groups of companies have been formed to develop personal digital assistants (PDAs). Apple developed its Newton using chips from Advanced RISC Machines and with design and manufacturing help from Sharp; Apple is now licensing its technology to other companies. AT&T joined with Olivetti, Marubeni, and Matsushita in launching EO, a start-up company that developed the PDA to be sold by the partners. Casio and Tandy developed their own PDA that uses software from GeoWorks; and Amstrad worked with Eden for its version of the product.

The Characteristics of Alliance Groups

The idea that individual companies can gain competitive advantage from banding together is not new. Japanese companies have long done so in their *keiretsu,* and U.S. and European companies did so in the cartels they created after World War I. Today's alliance groups, however, are something different.

Keiretsu companies have long-standing and broad-based relationships with one another. They tend to help one another in various ways and in multiple fields of business. In contrast, alliance groups are more focused, their purposes more strategic, and the roles of their members more narrowly tailored. Interwar cartels differ even more starkly from alliance groups. U.S. and European companies in the sugar, rubber, nitrogen, steel, aluminum, magnesium, incandescent lamp, and chemical industries banded together in industrywide cartels with the aim of allocating world markets. Their purpose was to suppress competition. In contrast, more than one group usually exists in any industry, and competition between or among the groups can be fierce.

An alliance group, then, is a collection of separate companies linked through collaborative agreements. Not all the companies in a group have to be linked directly to all the others. Some may be related only by virtue of their common ties to another network company or to a single sponsoring company. For example, the Mips group was structured precisely in this way, as were competing groups formed by Sun Microsystems, IBM, and Hewlett-Packard (H-P). All groups were created to promote the RISC (reduced instruction-set computing) technology of the sponsoring company. (See the exhibit, "The Structure of the RISC Groups.") There may be an overarching collaborative agreement to which all network members are party; most of the RISC groups had such agreements in place. But the point is that a constellation of alliances can consist of few or many companies. Indeed, alliance groups vary by size, pattern of growth, composition, internal competition, and governance structure. What's appropriate for one network might be wholly inappropriate for another.

SIZE

Alliance networks often grow out of the need to gain scale economies or market share. That was precisely

The Structure of the RISC Groups

Each group in the RISC computer field was composed of a mix of companies and types of alliances. The company at the center of each group usually designed the RISC technology, licensed the semiconductor companies to produce chips, and supplied systems on an OEM basis to the resellers. The link between the central company and the system manufacturers was often less formal: the latter simply committed to using the RISC design in their systems. Finally, some of the companies were linked to one another through equity investments.

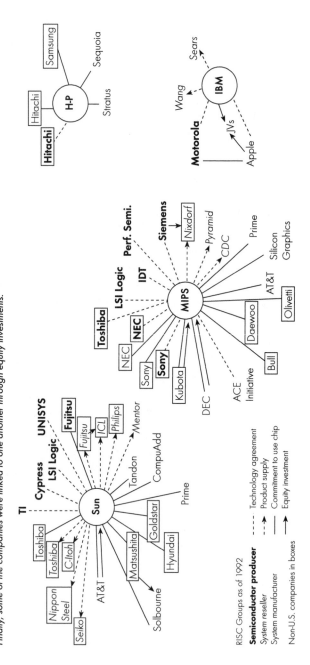

RISC Groups as of 1992

Semiconductor producer   ---- Technology agreement
System reseller   --▶ Product supply
System manufacturer   —— Commitment to use chip
                               —▶ Equity investment
Non-U.S. companies in boxes

Mips's objective in creating its RISC group. Mips sought
to challenge the likes of Intel, Motorola, Sun, and others,
each of which was developing its own design for a RISC
chip to be used in workstations. Mips turned to partnerships. Seeking strength in numbers, it licensed NEC,
Siemens, Toshiba, LSI Logic, and two smaller companies
to produce its chips; it persuaded Digital Equipment
Corporation (DEC), Silicon Graphics, Bull, Nixdorf,
Olivetti, and others to agree to use them; and it struck up
working relationships with a host of software companies,
system integrators, and computer resellers.

As Mips's network of alliances grew, Compaq and
Microsoft joined in, and the group launched a joint effort
to develop a new standard for personal computers, the
Advanced Computing Environment (ACE). Within
months, more than 150 companies had signed on to help.
Suddenly, Intel, IBM, Apple, H-P, and Sun were on
notice. To defend their own technologies, IBM, Motorola,
and Apple joined together in a group around the PowerPC chip, and Sun and H-P strengthened and expanded
their respective groups. Intel independently redoubled
its efforts to develop the Pentium chip, which would
compete with the RISC chip of Mips and others. Within a
year, the Mips juggernaut had been checked. Mips itself
was soon acquired by Silicon Graphics, and the ACE initiative died. But group-based competition in the industry
continues. The Mips network survives, and competition
among it and the groups headed by IBM, H-P, and Sun
remains strong.

When the competition among networks centers on
the establishment of an industry standard, the number
of companies in the network and their combined share
of the total market are critical to success. Sun recruited a
large number of companies to its technology. Mips's

competing network of alliances contained fewer, larger members. In their collective strengths, these two networks were roughly evenly matched, but IBM neutralized

Most alliance groups don't spring into life fully formed. They are built gradually, piece by piece.

the numerical advantage of Mips and Sun when it joined with Apple. The two personal computer giants together could promise a potentially huge market

share for PowerPC, the RISC technology microprocessor that IBM developed with Motorola.

Overall size may be less important in alliance networks driven by the convergence of two or more industries like those in the multimedia field. The idea here is to link complementary technologies or markets. Still, when the dissimilar partners in these alliance networks can exploit economies of scale in their own industries, a greater volume of joint business can help the network in its common purpose.

PATTERN OF GROWTH

Most alliance networks don't spring into existence fully formed; they are built piece by piece. Both the rate of growth and the sequence in which particular members join can affect a network's competitive success. For instance, Kubota, a Japanese machinery producer seeking to diversify into computers, provided Mips with capital at a critical stage and thereby supported the network's early growth. DEC's subsequent decision to join the group gave Mips credibility at a crucial time and led to the decision of NEC and Siemens to become Mips allies. This impressive core group then pulled other companies into the Mips orbit. Later, the addition of

Microsoft and Compaq was critical to the launching of
the ACE initiative.

Mips's experience suggests that groups can experience runaway growth that ultimately may not be sustainable. While the rapid growth of ACE was a public
relations coup for Mips, the large number of companies
involved hampered the effectiveness of the group. Competing interests existed even among the core group of
ACE founders, and additional conflicts emerged as new
companies joined. Consequently, Mips itself was pulled
in different directions, and the network soon showed
signs of fractures.

IBM pursued a more cautious growth strategy in
building the network of alliances that would develop and
market the PowerPC. First, it collected its main players
by creating close alliances with Apple and Motorola.
Apple's earlier ties with Motorola (its computers used
Motorola chips) helped cement the three-way network.
This triad was charged with developing the new semiconductor, hardware, and software technologies needed
for the PowerPC. Only then did IBM fan out to find other
players, such as Bull.

Two general principles about the process of growth
emerge from these examples. First, to attract new members, a network must show a potential for joint benefits.
Some companies will see the potential early, but more
skeptical companies may have to be convinced and will
only join later in the network's development. Often, the
very fact of network growth will attract cautious latecomers. Second, previous relationships between allies
and potential allies can be important in attracting new
members. Sometimes this means that an ally of an ally
will join the group or that an enemy of the enemy will
sign on.

COMPOSITION

In networks of companies in converging industries, more important than network size or business volume or even market share is composition—ensuring that the network covers all technologies or markets crucial to the product. The mix of companies in these groups tends to reflect the new opportunities that convergence offers for combining technologies. But even in well-established industries, where the intention is to match the skills assembled by competing networks, composition can be important to a network's success. Both the Ford and GM alliance networks, for instance, contain members with comparable skills and specialties—strong Japanese companies (Mazda with Ford, and Toyota with GM), European luxury-car makers (Jaguar and Saab), and European truck makers (Fiat and Volvo).

In standards battles, too, network composition matters. The leading companies in RISC technology designed their networks to include all the capabilities they thought they needed to compete. The differences in the mix of companies in these networks depended on the capabilities of the RISC designer itself. Neither Mips nor Sun fabricated its own semiconductor chips, so both allied themselves with a handful of semiconductor producers. Beyond that, however, the composition of their respective networks reflected the organizers' different needs. Sun was already successful at making and selling its own workstation systems, accounting for the bulk of RISC workstation sales in its network. Sun thus concentrated on adding OEM resellers and software producers to its network. Mips, in contrast, recruited more systems manufacturers and vendors. In order to help attract these systems companies, Mips even committed to limiting its own sales of finished systems. The composition of IBM's RISC network is different still. With little need for additional semiconductor and systems manufacturing capability beyond that of the triad core—IBM, Apple, and Motorola—IBM concentrated on adding software partners instead.

INTERNAL COMPETITION

The level of internal competition depends both on how many members perform similar functions and on the structure of the relationships among the members. Mips and Sun approached this issue very differently in their respective networks.

Mips licensed six semiconductor producers worldwide to make its R3000 microprocessor. This degree of duplication was intentional, as it helped assure customers that they would not become dependent on a single source. But, with it, Mips tried to minimize competition among its alliance partners: it licensed 6, not 60, producers and, in selecting them, tried to minimize potential rivalries in each company's geographic market. Sun, on the other hand, did little to discourage competition among its semiconductor suppliers. It tended to use a different supplier for each successive generation of its chip and let the suppliers compete each time for its business. Finally, H-P emphasized complementarity among a smaller number of allies than MIPS had. "This enables the partners to work

Collective governance ensures that a group is more than a haphazard collection of alliances.

together more smoothly rather than focus primarily on competing among themselves," explains Jim Bell, president of H-P's Precision RISC Organization, which helps coordinate H-P's alliances in the RISC field.

Internal competition has two opposing effects on performance. To a point, it increases group flexibility, drives innovation, and ensures security of supply. But it can fragment a part of the business so much that none of the members reaches efficient scales or earns a sufficient return to reinvest in growth. The line between just enough and too much competition is a fine one. Furthermore, different companies within any given network will have different opinions about where that line should be drawn. Companies subject to internal competition will opt for more order. Other network members may benefit, at least in the short run, from competition among suppliers or buyers inside the network.

GOVERNANCE STRUCTURE

Cooperation between companies is never automatic. The structure of the partnership must provide incentives for performance. Without some sort of collective governance, a group risks becoming no more than a haphazard collection of alliances.

One characteristic of a network's governance structure is the degree to which it is managed as a collective. At one extreme, many formal consortia have governing bodies composed of representatives from member companies, with no individual member in control. Sun's RISC group, for example, has created Sparc International to coordinate some of its efforts; IBM and its partners have created the Power Open Association; and H-P has created the Precision RISC Organization. But alliance networks may also function without joint management, as Mips's RISC group did. In these networks, member companies maintain a relationship to the lead company, thereby creating the larger group. The lead company usually provides the management for these multiple partnerships.

Group-Based Versus Company-Based Advantages

Who wins and who loses *among* competing alliance groups depends on the competitive advantages that each group of companies collectively builds. Who wins and who loses *within* a group is a related, but very different, matter. The executive who is considering joining or forming a network must be able to distinguish between group- and company-based advantages.

To attract new members, a network must show potential for joint benefits.

Group-based advantages help determine the success of the collective in relation to other groups. Company-based advantages, taken together, help the network compete by providing it with the components needed for success. Taken individually, these same company-based advantages help determine the position and power of each company within the network. In other words, if the network-based advantages create the total pie available to members, the company-based advantages affect how the pie is divided.

While group- and company-based advantages are thus intertwined, the balance between the two may in itself be a distinct element of a network. In some networks—Sun's, for example—a host of second-tier companies surrounds the central company that holds key advantages and owns the bulk of the collective business. In other networks—IBM's, for instance—a number of core companies holds complementary but equally critical advantages and shares the business more evenly. Both arrangements can work, and the choice may simply reflect the size of the organizing company or the companies in the core group.

These distinctions between group- and company-based advantages suggest three questions that managers should address as they design an alliance network:

- **Is the whole greater than the sum of its parts?** An alliance group works best when the individual partnerships complement one another or, at least, when they don't conflict. The network structure should provide incentives for member cooperation, not dissent.

- **Who controls the group?** The company that founds the group does not always remain in control. Small companies, in particular, run the risk of losing control to larger partners or to subgroups of partners within the network unless they own a critical part of the group's value chain. How the network is governed and how control is shared influence the effectiveness of the whole and the fate of individual members.

  Companies in groups should weigh the benefits of size against drawbacks like strategic gridlock and dependence.

- **Where is competitive advantage created?** The performance of a company within the group depends both on competitive advantages created by the group as a whole and on advantages of the company compared with other group members. The group-based advantages, in turn, depend on key characteristics of the group—size, composition, governance, internal competition, and processes of growth. Each company will gain competitive advantage according to the group it joins and the role it plays within that group.

The Hidden Costs of Alliance Groups

While increasing size may be an indication of a network's growing strength and success, size often comes at some expense. Companies building or participating in alliance networks should therefore weigh the benefits of greater size against three types of constraints.

Organizational constraints are internal to the company and weigh heaviest on the lead, or central, company in a network. Every new alliance requires top management's attention, especially in the early stages of planning, partner search, and negotiation. Every new alliance increases the difficulties of coordinating operations as more partners have to be consulted. In this sense, a network of alliances becomes more difficult to manage the more members it has. When partners have conflicting interests—in other words, when there is internal competition—the task of managing a network becomes still more difficult. When he was CEO of Mips in 1991 and trying to manage partnerships with NEC, Siemens, LSI Logic, Performance Semiconductor, and Integrated Device Technology, Robert Miller observed, "Keeping five companies on the same strategic path can be difficult; it takes diplomacy, time, and energy at the senior level."

While managers of large networks of alliances are currently struggling with how best to manage them, several models are beginning to show promise. Some companies have put a top executive in charge of over-seeing external strategic relations. These managers are often able to give their personal attention to only a small portion of the alliances within the network. Often they concentrate on alliances involving equity invest-ments while developing guidelines for the decentralized control of looser relationships.

Other companies allocate alliance responsibility along functional lines, such as marketing alliances under mar-keting executives or technology alliances under R&D departments. Still others require business units to man-age their own relationships. Particularly critical alliance networks are sometimes managed by specific senior-executive "champions," who may sit on the boards of joint ventures or otherwise take direct responsibility for alliance negotiation and management.

Collective governance structures such as IBM's Power Open Association and Sun's Sparc International may help maintain network cohesion. However, the burden of negotiating with new partners and monitoring existing agreements usually falls to the central company within the network. Therefore, top-level executives of the cen-tral company must always bear in mind that mismanage-ment can erode the group-based advantages that size and variety generate.

Strategic gridlock is external to the company, because it stems from crowding in the alliance field. As more partnerships are formed in a given business or country, there are likely to be fewer partners available for new deals. This constraint is particularly troublesome in oligopolistic industries, in which only a few strong com-panies compete world-wide. In the RISC field, for exam-ple, the early movers, Mips and Sun, tied up important partners in Europe and Japan. Fortunately for IBM and

DEC, by the time they decided to create their respective RISC networks, Mips's once extensive network had begun to decline and the ties among its members to weaken. As a result, IBM could attract Bull and Wang, and DEC could lure Olivetti.

These external limits on alliance strategies are not easy to manage, and most companies are trying one of three approaches: preemption, avoidance, or compartmentalization. First, partner scarcity often provokes companies to take preemptive strikes early in order to secure their first choices. As soon as alliances come to be seen as potentially useful in entering or dominating a field, leading companies may leap to create partnerships, sometimes on short notice and with a minimum of planning. Second, companies may avoid, when possible, taking on partners that might involve conflicts of interest with existing alliances. Mips sought semiconductor partners that did not have their own RISC projects, thereby eliminating Motorola and Advanced Micro Devices as potential partners. Third, companies limit the scope of collaboration in each alliance—for example, by limiting its geographic territory. This kind of compartmentalization solution minimizes overlap, leaving each alliance to operate more or less independently of the others. But the approach sacrifices the benefits that can spring from integration among alliances. Indeed, compartmentalization almost ensures that the value of a network will not exceed the value of the sum of its parts.

Dependence is inherent in networks. In all alliances, the allying companies lose some control. To the extent that I rely on you, my freedom to act independently of you is reduced. Cumulatively, the growth of a network of alliances may gradually and inexorably link an individual company's destiny to that of the network. If that occurs, the company may have to subordinate its own decisions to those of the network. And, ironically, even if the network is growing and capturing market share, the company may have to share a progressively greater portion of network profits just to attract or retain alliance partners.

Organizational constraints, strategic gridlock, and dependence all contributed to the decline of Mips and its once-promising network of alliances. But of the three constraints, dependence took the greatest toll. To gain more sponsors, Mips had to share potential profits from its technology with partners. Furthermore, Mips's fate came to depend on the success of ACE, which in turn hinged on the actions of several key members, including DEC and Compaq. The limits on Mips's ability to appropriate returns from its technology weakened the company's financial condition, which cast doubt on Mips's ability to survive and discouraged potential new allies. It also forced Mips to cut back on R&D, eroding its technological advantage. As soon as DEC and Compaq reduced their commitment to ACE in 1992, the group fell apart. Mips, as an independent company, went down with it. It was then acquired by Silicon Graphics.

Latecomers to the RISC field are trying to avoid the problems that plagued Mips. H-P, DEC, and IBM, entering the race after Mips and Sun had already created their large constellations, are building smaller and more manageable groups. Silicon Graphics, which inherited the Mips network, has refocused on nurturing a few key alliances in targeted market segments.

What the Pioneers Have Learned

Because even pioneers in the field are still learning how to initiate, build, and manage networks of alliances, much of what they are learning is specific to their own experience. Still, a few general lessons have emerged:

- **Groups are only as strong as the alliances within them: manage individual relationships carefully.** There is no shortcut to designing and implementing partnerships. Even when no new money is being spent, the task requires the same depth of analysis that managers typically apply to major investment decisions. (See Rosabeth Moss Kanter, "Collaborative Advantage: The Art of Alliances," Chapter 5).

- **Effective groups are worth more than the sum of the alliances within them: manage the group as a whole.** Anything less than explicit group management constitutes a lost opportunity to create competitive advantage. Opportunity costs can turn into real costs if a network is left untended and uncultivated.

- **The sky is not the limit in alliance groups: expand with caution.** The pressure to forge links with new partners is often great, particularly when one's competitors are doing so daily. However, beware of falling prey to a faddish exuberance. Expand an alliance network only when it makes strategic sense. Even then, do so with the organizational constraints mentioned above in mind.

- **Where you sit in which network determines what you get: position your company strategically within and among alliance groups.** This is the essence of network competition. Managers need to pay attention to both group- and company-based sources of competitive advantage.

- **A lack of commitment is the flip side of flexibility: be sure that the network strategy is sustainable for**

your company. Alliance groups can fall apart just as rapidly as they are formed. When rivalry among networks is great, competitors will think nothing of picking off the members of a network teetering on dissolution.

Managers who follow these guidelines will avoid some of the pitfalls of their predecessors. And their experiences, in turn, will help refine old ideas and develop new ones about how to manage competition among groups.

Originally published in July–August 1994
Reprint 94402

Collaborative Advantage:

The Art of Alliances

ROSABETH MOSS KANTER

Executive Summary

WHEN COMPANIES JOIN FORCES—whether on research or as full-scale partners—often the tendency is to emphasize the legal or financial aspects of the deal. But smart managers know that alliances involve much more. Like human relationships, business partnerships are living systems that have endless possibilities. And companies that know how to tap those possibilities, and manage alliances effectively, have a key corporate asset. Rosabeth Moss Kanter calls it a *collaborative advantage*.

After completing a study of more than 37 companies from 11 parts of the world, Kanter concludes that relationships between companies grow or fail much like relationships between people. In fact, they tend to develop in five phases, just like human relationships. First, during the courtship, commonalities and mutual needs bring companies together. Key at this stage is the creation and maintenance of a good personal relationship between senior executives. Next, formal plans are made, and other people get involved—professionals such as lawyers and accountants. But maintaining a balance between the personal and institutional is still important in this stage. Then, in the housekeeping phase, people on both sides must learn to live together. That takes a lot of communication, and the parties find new ways of working together (phase four). Finally, as old-marrieds, the partners live together comfortably—and find themselves changed internally.

By paying attention to the human aspects of alliances, managers can leverage the maximum value from them, Kanter believes. Examples of companies enjoying a collaborative advantage today are FCB and Publicis; Northern Telecom and Matra Hachette; and the European Retail Alliance partners, Ahold, Argyll, and Groupe Casino.

ALLIANCES BETWEEN COMPANIES, whether they are from different parts of the world or different ends of the supply chain, are a fact of life in business today. Some alliances are no more than fleeting encounters, lasting only as long as it takes one partner to establish a beachhead in a new market. Others are the prelude to a full merger of two or more companies' technologies and capabilities. Whatever the duration and objectives of business alliances, being a good partner has become a key corporate asset. I call it a company's *collaborative advantage.* In the global economy, a well-developed ability to create and sustain fruitful collaborations gives companies a significant competitive leg up.

Yet, too often, top executives devote more time to screening potential partners in financial terms than to managing the partnership in human terms. They tout the future benefits of the alliance to their shareholders but don't help their managers create those benefits. They worry more about controlling the relationship than about nurturing it. In short, they fail to develop their company's collaborative advantage and thereby neglect a key resource.

Three years ago, I began a worldwide quest for lessons about productive partnerships, especially but not exclusively those intercompany relationships that spanned two or more countries and cultures. My research group and I observed more than 37 companies and their partners from 11 parts of the world (the United States, Canada, France, Germany, the United Kingdom, the Netherlands, Turkey, China, Hong Kong, Indonesia, and Japan). We included large and small companies in both manufacturing and service industries that were involved in many kinds of alliances. To ensure that the lessons were widely applicable, we sought companies less prominent in the business press than giants like IBM, Corning, Motorola, or Ford. Several of the relationships that we studied were more than 20 years old; others had formed only recently in response to industry and geopolitical changes. In multiple visits, we conducted more than 500 interviews with leaders and staffs of both partners. Over time, we saw relationships blossom after good or rocky starts; change goals or structures; and wither or dissolve—amicably or contentiously. Our research uncovered three fundamental aspects of business alliances:

Business alliances are living systems, evolving progressively in their possibilities.

- They must yield benefits for the partners, but they are more than just the deal. They are living systems that evolve progressively in their possibilities. Beyond the immediate reasons they have for entering into a relationship, the connection offers the parties an option on the future, opening new doors and unforeseen opportunities.

- Alliances that both partners ultimately deem successful involve *collaboration* (creating new value together) rather than mere *exchange* (getting something back for what you put in). Partners value the skills each brings to the alliance.

- They cannot be "controlled" by formal systems but require a dense web of interpersonal connections and internal infrastructures that enhance learning.

Moreover, we observed that North American companies, more than others in the world, take a narrow, opportunistic view of relationships, evaluating them strictly in financial terms or seeing them as barely tolerable alternatives to outright acquisition. Preoccupied with the economics of the deal, North American companies frequently neglect the political, cultural, organizational, and human aspects of the partnership. Asian companies are the most comfortable with relationships, and therefore they are the most adept at using and exploiting them. European companies fall somewhere in the middle.

Exploring the different outcomes of the business relationships of other companies can help companies manage their own. Successful alliances build and improve a collaborative advantage by first acknowledging and then effectively managing the human aspects of their alliances.

Varieties of Relationships

Cooperative arrangements between companies range along a continuum from weak and distant to strong and close. At one extreme, in *mutual service consortia*, similar companies in similar industries pool their resources to gain a benefit too expensive to acquire alone—access to an advanced technology, for example. At mid-range, in *joint ventures*, companies pursue an opportunity that needs a capability from each of them—the technology of one and the market access of the other, for example. The joint venture might operate independently, or it might link the partners' operations. The strongest and closest collaborations are *value-chain partnerships*, such as supplier-customer relationships. Companies in different industries with different but complementary skills link their capabilities to create value for ultimate users. Commitments in those relationships tend to be high, the partners tend to develop joint activities in many functions, operations often overlap, and the relationship thus creates substantial change within each partner's organization.

Relationships between companies begin, grow, and develop—or fail— much like relationships between people.

Companies can participate simultaneously in many kinds of relationships, and partners in any relationship may play a variety of roles. The 65 partners in Inmarsat, a consortium that operates a telecommunications satellite, are simultaneously *owners* investing capital, *customers* routing calls through the satellites, *suppliers* of technology to the venture, *regulators* setting policy, and *competitors* offering services similar to Inmarsat's. Netas, Northern Telecom's joint venture with local investors in

Turkey, is simultaneously an *investment asset* for Northern, a *customer* for Northern equipment, a *supplier* of new software and systems, and a *gatekeeper* to other relationships.

In every case, a business relationship is more than just the deal. It is a connection between otherwise independent organizations that can take many forms and contains the potential for additional collaboration. It is a mutual agreement to continue to get together; thus its value includes the potential for a stream of opportunities.

Selection and Courtship

Relationships between companies begin, grow, and develop—or fail—in ways similar to relationships between people. (See "Eight I's That Create Successful We's" at the end of this article.) No two relationships travel the same path, but successful alliances generally unfold in five overlapping phases.

In the first—courtship—two companies meet, are attracted, and discover their compatibility. During the second—engagement—they draw up plans and close the deal. In phase three, the newly partnered companies, like couples setting up housekeeping, discover they have different ideas about how the business should operate. In phase four, the partners devise mechanisms for bridging those differences and develop techniques for getting along. And in phase five, as old-marrieds, each company discovers that it has changed internally as a result of its accommodation to the ongoing collaboration.

Like romances, alliances are built on hopes and dreams—what might happen if certain opportunities are pursued.

"Love at first sight?" "The company of our dreams?" In fact, many executives use romantic analogies to describe the enthusiasm that accompanies their discovery of a new corporate partner. "One of the reasons our alliance was consummated so quickly," reports a Foote, Cone & Belding executive about the Chicago ad agency's partnership with Paris-based Publicis SA, "was that it was . . . love at first sight."

Such analogies are appropriate because business pairings aren't entirely cold-blooded. Indeed, successful company relationships nearly always depend on the creation and maintenance of a comfortable personal relationship between the senior executives.

Alliances and partnerships are initially romantic in another sense: their formation rests largely on hopes and dreams—what might be possible if certain opportunities are pursued. Strategic and financial analyses contribute a level of confidence, but, like all new business ventures, collaborative relationships draw energy largely from the optimistic ambition of their creators. COMCO, a Swiss diversified services company, seeing a big demand for environmental cleanup in Eastern Europe, touted enthusiastically the benefits of its joint venture with the U.S. expert, Martech. COMCO optimistically made the Martech joint venture a linchpin of its future growth strategy and assumed Martech felt the same way. Only later, when a cash infusion was needed and Martech backed off, did COMCO realize that its infatuation had been one-sided. Eastern Europe was less important to Martech than it was to COMCO, and more remote; also, Martech had wanted quick returns.

The risk of missing a rare opportunity also motivates company leaders to enter into relationships with open-ended possibilities beyond just clear financial payoffs. For example, newly privatized telecommunications businesses in Europe, Latin America, and Asia often find many foreign companies bidding for their affections, even when financial payoffs are uncertain and venture strategies confusing. Those companies offer a rare chance for outsiders to acquire inside positions in country markets.

Furthermore, distance lends enchantment. Company leaders often don't know each other well enough to be aware of, never mind bothered by, a potential partner's subtle differences. Selective perceptions reinforce the dreams, not the dangers. Leaders see in the other what they want to see and believe what they want to believe, often realizing only later that infatuation blinded them to early warning signs. One leader on the European side of an alliance with a U.S. company blamed himself for believing that his country unit would become the lead center for both companies' products worldwide. "I was ignoring the fact that we were two separate companies," he says, "and that our partner would never accept part of its business being run by an outsider."

The selection process may go better if companies look for three key criteria:

1. *Self-analysis.* Relationships get off to a good start when partners know themselves and their industry, when they have assessed changing industry conditions and decided to seek an alliance. It also helps if executives have experience in evaluating potential partners. They won't be easily dazzled by the first good-looking prospect that comes along.

2. *Chemistry.* To highlight the personal side of business relationships is not to deny the importance of sound financial and strategic analyses. But deals often turn on rapport between chief executives. And the feel-

ings between them that clinch or negate a relationship transcend business to include personal and social interests. Also, a good personal rapport between executives creates a well of goodwill to draw on later if tensions develop.

Northern Telecom was not even on the list when Matra Hachette of France began to seek partners for its Matra Communication subsidiary. In late 1991, negotiations with Philips, Siemens, and AT&T were well under way when Northern chairman Paul Stern asked Matra chairman Jean-Luc Lagardère to consider his company. Eventually Matra executives flew to North America to meet Stern and other senior staff. Two weeks later, Stern flew to France to dine with Lagardère. Skeptical at first, Lagardère was won over. "Our views on business," Stern says, "were similar: speed, disdain for bureaucracy, a willingness to make decisions. We hit it off socially; we share an interest in the arts and fast cars." Northern also impressed Lagardère and other Matra managers because Stern got personally involved; CEOs from other companies had left all contact to lower functionaries. In July 1992, Northern and Matra closed the deal.

Signs of the leader's interest, commitment, and respect are especially important in certain countries. In China, as well as in Chinese-dominated businesses throughout Asia, company suitors should give "face" (honor and respect) to a potential partner's decision makers by investing the personal time of their own leaders.

3. *Compatibility*. The courtship period tests compatibility on broad historical, philosophical, and strategic grounds: common experiences, values and principles, and hopes for the future. While analysts examine financial viability, leaders can assess the less tangible aspects

of compatibility. When British retailer BhS decided to
form partnerships with a small number of key suppliers

*FCB and Publicis
had common goals: expand
internationally and
retain Nestlé as a client.*
instead of continuing its
"promiscuity" with many
suppliers, to use one executive's term, then CEO
David Dworkin met with
the head of each prospec-
tive partner to explore business philosophies—not products and finances.

The initial relationship building between ad agencies
Foote, Cone & Belding and Publicis involved the discovery of many commonalities. Publicis, operating in 39
major European cities by 1987, was twentieth in the
world in billings. FCB, also with an extensive international presence, ranked fifteenth. Both agencies shared
the same industry imperative—to improve their international reach—and the same important catalyst, the
announcement by Nestlé, a leading client of both, that it
would reduce its ad agencies from 100 to 5.

FCB and Publicis both brought humility to their
growth plans, which made them open to sharing control; each believed that it could not grow alone and that
industry globalization was blunting its competitive
edge. Both had searched for several years without finding the right partner, so they had sufficient experience
with other potential partners to be satisfied with what
they found in each other. Each company was strong in
territories that the other was not, but there was reasonable equivalence in the strengths each brought to the
relationship. The companies had similar creative principles and operating philosophies, similar experiences
with common clients, and few areas of direct business
conflict.

In 1987, "Nestlé told us it wanted five global agencies and that, unless we did something, we would not be one of them," Publicis managing director Gerard Pedraglio recalls. Meanwhile, he had tried to hire Antonio Beja to manage the company's Spanish operations. Though Beja did not take the offer, the two men stayed in touch. Beja eventually became head of Asian and Latin American operations for FCB. In December 1987, Beja and Pedraglio met for dinner, and in the course of their conversation, Beja described his chairman's strategy for FCB. Pedraglio interrupted. "Now, Antonio," he said, "You stop, and I will finish." He did, and Beja was astounded. "How did you know?" he asked. "That's our plan too," Pedraglio replied.

Beja told FCB chairman Norman Brown about his dinner discussion with Pedraglio, and soon after that, Publicis representatives were on a plane to Chicago. Six months and five meetings later, having seen in each other a fulfillment of their needs, Publicis and FCB announced their alliance. "We found early on a remarkable degree of similarity in our creative and operating philosophies," an FCB executive explains.

The results of their collaboration confirm those findings. Since 1988, Publicis and FCB have operated an innovative global alliance and built a network of 173 agencies in 43 countries. Together the partners constitute the second largest agency in Europe, the second largest in North America, and the eighth largest in the world.

The FCB-Publicis alliance is evidence that, especially in fast-moving industries, potential partners must find compatibility in legacy, philosophy, and desires, because specific opportunities are often short-lived and won't sustain a long-term relationship. A relationship that falters or fails as soon as the first project is concluded precludes other opportunities from developing. Moreover, side deals can quickly become significant in a sustained relationship. The potential to tap Matra Communication's cellular radio technologies was a side benefit of Northern Telecom's alliance with Matra Hachette. Within a year, the side benefit had become the most important and productive piece of the alliance.

Powersoft entered into an alliance with Lotus to share manufacturing space and soon discovered that sharing Lotus's new packaging technology was even more valuable. Inmarsat's original maritime communications venture, which joined partners such as Comsat, British Telecom, Teleglobe, and Japan's KDD, has been dwarfed in growth potential by newer activities in aeronautical and land mobile communications. For TechRidge, a small manufacturer of specialized cameras for identification card photos, a long-standing relationship with Polaroid took a new turn when a Polaroid ally included Polaroid in a large contract in Mexico, and Polaroid brought along TechRidge. This unanticipated opportunity gave TechRidge a platform for further globalization.

Sometimes, particularly in Asia, partners are selected more for their potential to open future doors than for immediate benefits. Lippo Group, a rapidly growing financial conglomerate, has tapped a network of Japanese, European, and U.S. partners to expand from its Indonesian home base to Hong Kong and China. Founder and chairman Mochtar Riady believes that promising relationships should be nurtured for their future value, even when initial joint ventures are not very profitable.

Many relationships die an early death when they are scrutinized for quick returns. COMCO's alliance with

Martech for environmental cleanup services in Eastern Europe dissolved in less than two years because of disputes over slower-than-expected returns and the need for new investment, even though the market potential was still great.

Getting Engaged

What starts out as personal rapport, philosophical and strategic compatibility, and shared vision between two companies' top executives eventually must be institutionalized and made public. Other stakeholders get involved, and the relationship begins to become depersonalized. But success in the engagement phase of a new alliance still depends on maintaining a careful balance between the personal and the institutional.

MEETING THE FAMILY

The rapport between chief executives and a handful of company leaders must be supplemented by the approval, formal or informal, of other people in the companies and of other stakeholders. Also, each partner has other outside relationships that need to approve of the new tie: government ministries, major customers and suppliers, other partners, and investors. Sometimes those meetings don't go well.

In the early stages of an alliance in Europe, a French company representative took his U.S. counterpart to meet with a French government official in a ministry that had partial oversight of the deal. The U.S. manager proceeded to lecture the French official, a socialist, about the virtues of free-market capitalism. French leaders pride themselves on their intellect, so both the form and the substance of the meeting created significant problems. Later, the French managers had to smooth things over at the ministry and educate the American on appropriate behavior.

THE VOWS

Third-party professionals—lawyers, investment bankers, and their staffs—play their most important roles at this point in the process. But if they dominate, the relationship can become too depersonalized and lose the leaders' vision. It is important to remember that outside professionals don't have to live with the results of their work. Also, because of their professional bias, they are less likely to be interested in the symbolic substance of relationship building: the gestures of respect or the mutual give-and-take that cement a relationship.

One alliance between a U.S. company and a French company in the North Sea oil fields involved a few perfunctory meetings between the chief executives. Then the legal, financial, and strategy staffs took over under the guidance of external law firms. The alliance collapsed in just three years. The professionals were savvy about finance and contracts but not about what it would take to operate the joint venture or whether the two companies were operationally compatible. When the U.S. company later formed a productive alliance with a Dutch company, executives and key managers spent a great deal of time together discussing principles as well as specific agreements; lawyers' and analysts' roles were minimized.

The best agreements between companies contain three important components. First, they incorporate a specific joint activity, a first-step venture or project. This project makes the relationship real in practice, helps the partners learn to work together, and provides a basis for measuring performance. Having real work to do makes it possible to get the relationship started; the longer a courtship drags on without consummation, the more likely conditions or minds or both can change and jeopardize it.

Second, the vows should include a commitment to expand the relationship through side bets such as equity swaps or personnel exchanges. Such a commitment reflects a willingness to connect the fates of the companies, as in the European Retail Alliance, formed in 1989 by three large food retailers: Ahold in the Netherlands, Argyll in the United Kingdom, and Groupe Casino in France. The ERA collaboration gives partners low-cost opportunities for scale efficiencies and innovation. To cement the relationship, the partners bought modest amounts of one another's stock. The three ERA partners sell products to one another and collaborate in joint projects in insurance, data processing, hardware purchasing, quality assurance, and personnel development. They have also developed an 11-company marketing association based in Switzerland that works closely with manufacturers on product development.

ERA has enlarged each member's international supply base by sharing relationships already tested by another ERA company. These new alliances, in turn, provide new product offerings that enhance the companies' reputations as taste leaders in their home markets. For example, Argyll's Safeway stores bought 320,000 cases of wine from Casino for their 1992 Christmas promotion; Casino used Safeway suppliers in the United Kingdom to introduce Scottish smoked salmon products and other high-quality U.K. fresh foods to French consumers. Safeway's store-of-the-future, which opened in Edinburgh in November 1993, features ERA-derived concepts new to the U.K. market—French-style delis, for example. ERA also helps its partners test future opportunities that might emerge as Europe integrates further. Argyll's chairman, Sir Alistair Grant, stresses ERA's long-term benefits: "Perhaps above all, the Retail Alliance has helped our team to become serious about Europe. I believe that our successors will be grateful for this." Externally, ERA opens borders. Inside member companies, it opens minds.

Third, the vows should incorporate clear signs of continuing independence for all partners. The FCB-Publicis alliance appointed an American as chairman of the European joint venture, so FCB's European staff and clients wouldn't think FCB was ceding its European operations to its French partner. When Matra allied with Northern Telecom, it preserved continuity in its product lines, even at the price of duplication with Northern products, to show customers that it would continue to upgrade and service installed machines.

Setting Up Housekeeping

The romance of courtship quickly gives way to day-to-day reality as partners begin to live together. Joint ventures are also new ventures and are thus fraught with uncertainty and unanticipated roadblocks. Now more than just the upper echelons of management must work together to make the partnership succeed.

PROBLEMS OF BROADER INVOLVEMENT

As actual projects get under way, many more people filling many more roles must work with members of the other organization. This broader involvement threatens to undermine the commitment forged at the top, for four reasons:

1. People in other positions may not experience the same attraction and rapport as the chief executives did. For example, during their alliance's early years, Publicis and FCB top executives maintained close contact, traveling often to each other's headquarters. They spent a lot of time together both informally and formally. Other employees had not been in touch with one another, however, and in some cases had to be pushed to work with their overseas counterparts.

2. Employees at other levels in the organization may be less visionary and cosmopolitan than top managers and less experienced in working with people from different cultures. They may lack knowledge of the strategic context in which the relationship makes sense and see only the operational ways in which it does not. For example, a member of the team developing a new financial product to be launched with a foreign partner complained repeatedly to his boss about the risks inherent in the product and the difficulties in introducing it, even recommending termination of the venture. He didn't realize that the foreign partner was a key gatekeeper for a lucrative development deal in another country. Senior managers were tolerating this risky venture in the hope of a larger payoff elsewhere.

3. Usually only a few staff people are dedicated full-time to the relationship. Others are evaluated on the performance of their primary responsibilities and therefore often neglect duties relating to the new alliance. Venture managers, more concerned about their

future in the parent company that appointed them, often give priority to their own company's events or executives and subordinate those of the partner.

4. People just one or two tiers from the top might oppose the relationship and fight to undermine it. This is especially true in organizations that have strong independent business units or among professional groups whose incentives aren't aligned with the interests of the organization as a whole. For example, a health care services company formed an alliance with a group of hospitals to create a single new facility to replace duplicate capacity in the hospitals. All the hospitals invested in the alliance, and the services company assumed they would bring enough business to make the venture profitable quickly. But that assumption proved wrong. While the hospital heads had committed to the relationship, they had ignored the views and needs—and the power—of the staff at the units to be closed. The staffs fought back. They cited issues about quality for not sending business to the new venture, and because it was having start-up problems, their claims were plausible. They also cut the transfer prices to internal customers to win their backing in keeping their units alive. And they neglected to send their people to work with the venture, which began to hemorrhage money badly. Eventually the alliance folded.

DISCOVERY OF DIFFERENCE

Operational and cultural differences emerge after collaboration is under way. They often come as a surprise to those who created the alliance. That failure could reflect blind spots on the part of the legal and financial analysts who dominate the engagement period, but even operating people see the similarities more often than the dissimilarities in potential partners. Experience has a way of opening their eyes.

Differences in authority, reporting, and decision making styles become noticeable at this stage in the new alliance: what people get involved in decisions; how quickly decisions are made; how much reporting and documentation are expected; what authority comes with a position; and which functions work together.

Before the alliance, for example, Publicis was a 75% privately held company whose chief executive dominate strategic decisions. FCB was a public company with a large number of senior managers trying to operate by consensus and generating a lot of paperwork: reports, financial statements, and lengthy meeting minutes. One key U.S. manager, who worked slowly through others according to a philosophy of empowerment, was regarded as weak by the French, who were used to a more directive style. Early in the relationship, some U.S. managers found Publicis too hierarchical, but some French managers found FCB's frequent meetings and paperwork too bureaucratic. And the French managers' abstractions and penchant for theory contrasted with the Americans' desire for concrete empirical facts.

Operational dissimilarities require working out— more communication than anyone could have anticipated.

Differences in structuring authority can have immediate practical consequences. In China, a chief engineer reports typically to the chief executive, whereas in

Canada, at Northern Telecom, he or she reports to the manufacturing director. Numerous other logistical and operational differences are soon discovered to be hiding behind the assumed compatibility: different product development schedules, views of the sales process, or technical standards, for example. Also, when the partners extend their areas of collaboration, the relationship becomes more difficult to govern and to evaluate on a purely financial basis.

The most common conflicts in relationships occur over money: capital infusions, transfer pricing, licensing fees, compensation levels, and management fees. Also, the complexity of roles each partner has with respect to the other can make economic decisions difficult. Remember, the relationship is larger than any one venture.

All operational dissimilarities require working out. More communication than anyone anticipated is necessary, and different languages make things even harder. In a Franco-American joint venture, meetings were conducted in both languages and thus took twice as long. Differences between companies do not disappear because of an alliance, but they can be handled so they don't jeopardize it. Companies that are good at partnering take the time to learn about the differences early and take them into account as events unfold.

RESPECT VERSUS RESENTMENT

People will take the time to understand and work through partnership differences to the extent that they feel valued and respected for what they bring to the relationship. Using stereotypes to explain people's behavior—the French always do this, or the Germans always do that, for example—denigrates individuals and therefore diminishes their incentive to bridge troubling differences.

Stereotyping polarizes the partners, setting up us-versus-them dynamics that undermine the desire to collaborate. One North American manager observed soon after forming an alliance with a European company, "You're an ugly American to them, backwater folks from across the pond, here to purchase, steal, whatever." A cynical countryman wondered whether the European partner's motive was to push the North American company out of the market.

Mistrust, once introduced, sets off a vicious cycle. It makes success harder to attain, which means someone has to be blamed for the lack of success. Because of their differences, outsiders are the most suspect—a fact that only increases mistrust. Respect that builds trust begins with an assumption of equality: all parties bring something valuable to the relationship and deserve to be heard. In one alliance, tension began to build after the local partner felt shut out of decisions, even though local knowledge was vital to the venture's success. A Chinese manager commented on the resentment that Western companies create when they assume that their superior technology gives them the right to make all the decisions. "The focus here," the manager said, "is on face, reputation. Even if people are poor, you need to give them face. North Americans feel that because they gave us jobs, we can't argue. But the Chinese people don't need their jobs. We can replace them with another foreign company; we can import from another place."

Learning to Collaborate

Active collaboration takes place when companies develop mechanisms—structures, processes, and skills—for bridging organizational and interpersonal differences and achieving real value from the partnership. Multiple ties at multiple levels ensure communication, coordination, and control. Deploying more rather than fewer people to relationship activities helps ensure that both partners' resources are tapped and that both companies' own needs and goals are represented.

The most productive relationships achieve five levels of integration:

1. *Strategic integration*, which involves continuing contact among top leaders to discuss broad goals or changes in each company. Leaders should not form an alliance and then abandon its nurturing to others. The more contact top executives have, the more changes they will hear about, the more chances they will have to work things out, the more information they will be able to turn into benefits, and the greater the possibility that the companies will evolve in complementary rather than conflicting directions.

Often, new governance forums evolve after the relationship is under way. The chief executives in the European Retail Alliance devote a day a month to their meetings, rotating among the three countries. Investment bankers Wertheim of the United States and Schroders of the United Kingdom began their alliance in 1986 with infrequent board meetings but soon saw the need for broader and more frequent contact. FCB and Publicis built their Alliance Operating Committee after realizing that having the CEOs sit on each other's boards didn't produce enough communication.

2. *Tactical integration*, which brings middle managers or professionals together to develop plans for specific projects or joint activities, to identify organizational or system changes that will link the companies better, or to transfer knowledge.

The ERA developed projects in insurance, information technology, and transportation that involved staff from member companies. Leadership for each project came from the company with the most experience or the best practices in that area. Northern Telecom and Matra Communication pinpointed four product domains in which potential synergies existed. Then they created four working groups of eight to ten people that met monthly to define specific ways of cooperating in each area. Members of all four groups convened in a general assembly every three months to report progress and problems to management. The small British apparel supplier Cohen & Wilks and its large retail partner, BhS, developed joint planning projects, including team efforts to improve computer linkups and financing mechanisms, such as a proposed retrospective discount scheme. BhS buying director Liz Broughan meets frequently with Cohen & Wilks staff members to plan product designs.

Establishing formal integrator roles is another way to ensure tactical integration. Lotus, Powersoft, and other partner-rich software companies have senior executives dedicated to alliance management, equivalent in status to the heads of finance or human resources. Worldwide account directors (WWADs) at FCB and Publicis work to make the best use of all resources of both partners on behalf of major clients. That task is complicated by another dynamic, the fact that each client relationship is very different. Some have highly centralized global marketing efforts; others give companies or regions autonomy to develop their own. Salomon Salto, WWAD for the FCB-Publicis relationship with Nestlé, communicates ideas to all parties but also intervenes in local conflicts. He is viewed as an impartial observer with experience in many countries and brands. "My job is more diplomacy and negotiation than power," he observes. His ability to speak French, Spanish, English, and German helps a lot.

3. *Operational integration*, which provides ways for people carrying out the day-to-day work to have timely access to the information, resources, or people they need to accomplish their tasks. Participation in each other's training programs helped two companies in a technology-based relationship develop a common vocabulary and product development standards. Computer connections between Cohen & Wilks and BhS provide direct data interchange, which speeds product development and delivery cycles. Inmarsat engineers in London share a technical vocabulary and systems with counterparts at the earth stations where partners receive satellite signals.

4. *Interpersonal integration*, which builds a necessary foundation for creating future value. As relationships mature beyond the early days of scrambling to create initial projects and erect structural scaffolding to manage them, the network of interpersonal ties between members of the separate companies grows in extent and density. Leaders soon feel the need to bring people together to share information. FCB and Publicis first expanded their initial Alliance Operating Committee to include more people. They then initiated worldwide conferences for executives and country managers. Next, they brought creative directors and account managers from both companies and many countries together to make recommendations for business development, creative excellence, and international client management.

Establishing many interpersonal relationships between partners helps resolve small conflicts before they escalate.

Broad synergies born on paper do not develop in practice until many people in both organizations know one another personally and become willing to make the effort to exchange technology, refer clients, or participate on joint teams. Lippo Group, which has many partners involved in its network of banks and property development ventures, uses senior management conferences to sell the concept of synergy, identify cross-unit business opportunities, and build personal ties among managers.

Many strong interpersonal relationships help resolve small conflicts before they escalate. "There really is no good system for working out problems except through personal relationships," observes a European manager experienced in transatlantic relationships. "If you don't establish good rapport with your counterparts, you haven't got a prayer of making it work. Formal structures of decision making don't do anything for you unless you've got the relationship to start with."

5. *Cultural integration*, which requires people involved in the relationship to have the communication skills and cultural awareness to bridge their differences. Northern Telecom and Matra picked executives for their Matra Northern Cellular joint venture who had shared a similar foreign assignment. Chief executive Émile Gratton is a bilingual Canadian who had worked in the United States, South America, and Saudi Arabia. Chief operating officer Olivier de Pazzis, deployed by Matra in France, had run a joint venture with a U.S. company in Saudi Arabia.

Managers from both partners or affiliated companies must become teachers as well as learners. Managers at Tong Guang Nortel, the successful venture in China between Tong Guang Electronics and Northern Telecom, have committed themselves to teaching and learning.

TGNT managing director Gerry Jones, deployed from the Northern side, arranged for Chinese deputy managing director Frank Yong to participate in a three-month training program in Canada to become familiar with Western business practices. That experience enabled Yong to raise questions with Northern managers in China and educate them about how situations appeared from the Chinese side of the venture. In turn, Yong arranged for his Western partners to visit important Chinese historic sites, such as the Great Wall and the Summer Palace, and invited them to Chinese weddings and to employees' homes.

When managers accept teaching and learning roles, they demonstrate interest and respect, which helps build the goodwill that's so useful in smoothing over cultural and organizational differences. TGNT's Canadian manufacturing director learned to speak Mandarin. Although he could hold only a simple conversation in Chinese, the enthusiastic applause he received at quarterly meetings in Shekou attested to his popularity. An American expatriate heading part of Lippo Group's insurance joint ventures knew that his primary job was to teach local managers analytic skills, but he also took the time to set up classes for himself and other expatriates to learn the local language and customs.

Integration in all five of these dimensions—strategic, tactical, operational, interpersonal, and cultural—requires that each party be willing to let the other parties inside, which entails a risk: the risk of change.

Changing Within

Productive relationships usually require and often stimulate changes within the partners, changes that they may not anticipate at the outset of the collaboration. When two companies place themselves in intimate contact with each other through an alliance, it is almost inevitable that each will compare itself with the other: How do we measure up to our partner in systems sophistication or operational efficiency? What lessons can we learn from our partner? In fact, learning and borrowing ideas from partners is part of realizing the full value of the relationship. FCB and Publicis used the formation of their alliance as the occasion to rethink the nature of an advertising agency and to create new roles for regional and country managers as well as for worldwide account directors.

EMPOWERMENT OF RELATIONSHIP MANAGERS

Because collaborative ventures often make new demands, managers involved in the relationship must be able to vary their own companies' procedures to make venture-specific decisions. Staff involved in alliance activities often need more knowledge and skills. When British retailer BhS established partnerships with suppliers like Cohen & Wilks, buyers on both sides needed new strategic and financial information and negotiating skills to work effectively with one another. One success factor in Northern Telecom's joint ventures in Turkey and China is the autonomy of each venture's board of directors and expatriate managers, an autonomy that allows them to depart from the practices the company follows in North American markets. In China, the ability to adapt to local markets—for example, in accounts receivable policies or incentive schemes for sales personnel—helped TGNT succeed. Developing flexibility—

"letting go," as one manager describes it—may be diffi-cult for tightly managed companies with detail-oriented managers.

INFRASTRUCTURE FOR LEARNING

Companies with strong communications across func-tions and widely shared information tend to have more productive external relationships. Thus other desirable internal changes include greater cross-functional team-work and exchange of ideas. At BhS, cross-functional teamwork is crucial for achieving the speed, innovation, and quality the company seeks from supplier partner-ships. Liz Broughan had to build bridges to marketing director Helena Packshaw and trading manager Sandee Springer.

Many businesses fail to realize the full potential from their relationships because internal barriers to commu-nication limit learning to the small set of people directly involved in the relationship. One large U.S. company's highest award for quality went to a joint venture operat-ing in a developing country, yet managers in that venture had a hard time convincing their colleagues in other countries that they had anything to teach them.

The company's systems are usually the culprit in such situations, not its people. In the early stages of its rela-tionship with Northern Telecom, Matra learned that Northern put designs into production earlier than Matra did. Despite a common stereotype that speed is less important in France, the French engineers rose quickly to the challenge and proudly demonstrated a new capa-bility several months ahead of schedule.

Specific forums to exchange ideas can help companies import lessons from their partners. In addition to top management's participation in the ERA, Argyll's Safeway stores have created a regional managers' forum and a senior executive development program. Cross-functional projects, such as offering discounts to customers who buy combinations of products, link marketing, information technology, and stores.

Managing the Trade-offs

There are limits to how much a company should change to accommodate the demands of an alliance. The potential value of the relationship must be weighed against the value of all the other company activities, which also make demands on its resources—including the time and energy of executives. Even when relationships have high value, an organization can handle only so many before demands begin to conflict and investment requirements (management time, partner-specific learning, capital, and the like) outweigh perceived benefits. (See Benjamin Gomes-Casseres, "Group Versus Group: How Alliance Networks Compete," Chapter 4.)

Sometimes companies must face the challenge of terminating an alliance. Relationships can end for a number of reasons. A partner may be suitable for one purpose and not another. Managers or other venture participants may be needed for more urgent tasks. Shifts in business conditions or strategy can mean that a particular relationship no longer fits as well as it once did. For whatever reason, ending a partnership properly is difficult to do and requires much skill and diplomacy. Partners should be fully informed and treated with integrity. If they are not, future relationships will be jeopardized—especially in Asian countries, where business and government leaders have long memories.

Like all living systems, relationships are complex. While they are simpler to manage when they are narrow in scope and the partners remain at arm's length, relationships like these yield fewer long-term benefits. Tighter control by one partner or development of a single command center might reduce conflicts and increase the manageability of a relationship. Many benefits, however, derive from flexibility and being open to new possibilities. Alliances benefit from establishing multiple, independent centers of competence and innovation. Each center can pursue different paths, creating in turn new networks that go off in new directions. Flexibility and openness bring particular advantages at business frontiers—in rapidly changing or new markets or in new technology fields.

The effective management of relationships to build collaborative advantage requires managers to be sensitive to political, cultural, organizational, and human issues. In the global economy today, companies are known by the company they keep. As the saying goes, success comes not just from what you know but from who you know. Intercompany relationships are a key business asset, and knowing how to nurture them is an essential managerial skill.

Eight I's That Create Successful We's

THE CHARACTERISTICS OF effective intercompany relationships challenge many decades of Western economic and managerial assumptions. For example, most Westerners assume that modern industrial companies are run best by professional managers operating within limited, contractual Western obligations. And most

Westerners assume that any person with the requisite knowledge, skills, and talents can be a manager in the modern corporation. Although smaller companies, family businesses, and companies that are operating in developing countries have retained "premodern" characteristics, the "rational" model has been considered the ideal to which all organizations would eventually conform.

Intercompany relationships are different. They seem to work best when they are more familylike and less rational. Obligations are more diffuse, the scope for collaboration is more open, understanding grows between specific individuals, communication is frequent and intensive, and the interpersonal context is rich. The best intercompany relationships are frequently messy and emotional, involving feelings like chemistry or trust. And they should not be entered into lightly. Only relationships with full commitment on all sides endure long enough to create value for the partners.

Indeed, the best organizational relationships, like the best marriages, are true partnerships that tend to meet certain criteria:

Individual Excellence. Both partners are strong and have something of value to contribute to the relationship. Their motives for entering into the relationship are positive (to pursue future opportunities), not negative (to mask weaknesses or escape a difficult situation).

Importance. The relationship fits major strategic objectives of the partners, so they want to make it work. Partners have long-term goals in which the relationship plays a key role.

Interdependence. The partners need each other. They have complementary assets and skills. Neither can accomplish alone what both can together.

Investment. The partners invest in each other (for example, through equity swaps, cross-ownership, or mutual board service) to demonstrate their respective stakes in the relationship and each other. They show tangible signs of long-term commitment by devoting financial and other resources to the relationship.

Information. Communication is reasonably open. Partners share information required to make the relationship work, including their objectives and goals, technical data, and knowledge of conflicts, trouble spots, or changing situations.

Integration. The partners develop linkages and shared ways of operating so they can work together smoothly. They build broad connections between many people at many organizational levels. Partners become both teachers and learners.

Institutionalization. The relationship is given a formal status, with clear responsibilities and decision processes. It extends beyond the particular people who formed it, and it cannot be broken on a whim.

Integrity. The partners behave toward each other in honorable ways that justify and enhance mutual trust. They do not abuse the information they gain, nor do they undermine each other.

Originally published in July–August 1994
Reprint 94405

The author acknowledges Pamela Yatsko, Paul Myers, Kalman Applbaum, Lisa Gabriel, Madelyn Yucht, and Gina Quinn, who collaborated on the research. Pamela Yatsko made especially important contributions.

Saving the Business Without Losing the Company

CARLOS GHOSN

Executive Summary

WHEN RENAULT AND NISSAN entered into a strategic alliance in March 1999, Nissan was in trouble. The Japanese automaker had been struggling for eight years to turn a profit. Its margins were notoriously low, and purchasing costs were 15% to 25% higher at Nissan than at Renault. Adding to the cost burden was a plant capacity far in excess of the company's needs: The Japanese factories alone could produce almost a million more cars a year than the company sold. And the company's debts, even after the Renault investment, amounted to more than $11 billion. This was, quite literally, a do-or-die situation: Either Nissan would turn the business around, or it would cease to exist. A veteran of turnarounds at Renault and Michelin, Carlos Ghosn was asked by Renault's CEO to go to Tokyo to save Nissan. He faced an uphill battle as a non-Japanese, non-Nissan outsider—and he knew it.

In this first-person account, Ghosn tells the story of Nissan's turnaround. He explains how he relied on cross-functional teams and how they became a powerful tool for getting line managers to see beyond functional and regional boundaries. Ghosn also contends that success is not simply a matter of making fundamental changes to a company's organization and operations; the company's identity and the self-esteem of its people must also be protected. Those two goals—making changes and safeguarding identity—can easily come into conflict; pursuing them both requires a difficult and sometimes precarious balancing act. The keys, he says, is to nurture a strong corporate culture that taps into the productive aspects of a country's culture.

IT WAS IN MARCH OF 1999 that I got the call from Louis Schweitzer, CEO of Renault, asking me if I would be willing to go to Tokyo to lead a turnaround at Nissan, the struggling Japanese motor giant. The two companies had just agreed to a major strategic alliance in which Renault would assume $5.4 billion of Nissan's debt in return for a 36.6% equity stake in the Japanese company. The combined company would be the world's fourth largest carmaker. On paper, the deal made sense for both sides: Nissan's strength in North America filled an important gap for Renault, while Renault's cash reduced Nissan's mountain of debt. The capabilities of the two companies were also complementary: Renault was known for innovative design and Nissan for the quality of its engineering.

The alliance's success, though, depended on turning Nissan into a profitable and growing business, which was what Schweitzer was calling on me to do. I suppose I was a natural candidate for the job, as I had just finished contributing to the turnaround initiative at Renault in the aftermath of its failed merger with Volvo. We had had to make some controversial decisions about European plant closures, difficult for a French company with a tradition of state control. I had been in challenging situations before then as well. In the 1980s, as COO of Michelin's Brazilian subsidiary, I had to contend with runaway inflation rates. In 1991, as the unit CEO of Michelin North America, I faced the task of putting together a merger with Uniroyal Goodrich, the U.S. tire company, just as the market went into a recession.

But Nissan was something else entirely. It had been struggling to turn a profit for eight years. Its margins were notoriously low; specialists estimated that Nissan gave away $1,000 for every car it sold in the United States due to the lack of brand power. Purchasing costs, I was soon to discover, were 15% to 25% higher at Nissan than at Renault. Further adding to the cost burden was a plant capacity far in excess of the company's needs: The Japanese factories alone could produce almost a million more cars a year than the company sold. And the company's debts, even after the Renault investment, amounted to more than $11 billion (for the convenience of our readers, the approximate exchange rate at the end of September 2001 of 120 yen to the U.S. dollar is used throughout). This was, quite literally, a do-or-die situation: Either we'd turn the business around or Nissan would cease to exist.

It was also an extremely delicate situation. In corporate turnarounds, particularly those related to mergers or alliances, success is not simply a matter of making fundamental changes to a company's organization and operations. You also have to protect the company's identity and the self-esteem of its people. Those two goals—making changes and safeguarding identity—can easily come into conflict; pursuing them both entails a difficult and sometimes precarious balancing act. That was particularly true in this case. I was, after all, an outsider—non-Nissan, non-Japanese—and was initially met with skepticism by the company's managers and employees. I knew that if I tried to dictate changes from above, the effort would backfire, undermining morale and productivity. But if I was too passive, the company would simply continue its downward spiral.

Today, less than three years later, I am pleased to report that the turnaround is succeeding. Nissan is profitable again, and its identity as a company has grown stronger. How did we manage it? In two key ways. First, rather than impose a plan for the company's revival, I mobilized Nissan's own managers, through a set of cross-functional teams, to identify and spearhead the radical changes that had to be made. Second, Renault remained sensitive to Nissan's culture at all times, allowing the company room to develop a new corporate culture that built on the best elements of Japan's national culture. In the following pages, I'll discuss the turnaround process and Nissan's new culture in more detail. But to really understand the Nissan story, you first have to understand how dramatically the company has broken with its past.

Breaking with Tradition

When I arrived at Nissan at the close of the 1990s, established business practices were wreaking huge damage on the company. Nissan was strapped for cash, which prevented it from making badly needed investments in its aging product line. Its Japanese and European entry-level car, the March (or the Micra in Europe), for example, was nearly nine years old. The competition, by contrast, debuted new products every five years; Toyota's entry-level car at the time was less than two years old. The March had had a few face-lifts over the years, but essentially we were competing for 25% of the Japanese market and a similar chunk of the European market with an old—some would say out-of-date—product. Similar problems plagued the rest of our car lines.

The reason Nissan had cut back on product development was quite simple: to save money. Faced with persistent operating losses and a growing debt burden, the company was in a permanent cash crunch. But it didn't have to be that way. Nissan actually had plenty of capital—the problem was it was locked up in noncore financial and real-estate investments, particularly in *keiretsu* partnerships. The keiretsu system is one of the enduring features of the Japanese business landscape. Under the system, manufacturing companies maintain equity stakes in partner companies. This, it's believed, promotes loyalty and cooperation. When the company is large, the portfolio can run to billions of dollars. When I arrived at Nissan, I found that the company had more than $4 billion invested in hundreds of different companies.

The problem was that the majority of these shareholdings were far too small for Nissan to have any managerial leverage on the companies, even though the sums involved were often quite large. For instance, one of Nissan's investments was a $216 million stake in Fuji Heavy Industries, a company that, as the manufacturer of Subaru cars and trucks, competes with Nissan. What sense did it make for Nissan to tie up such a large sum of money in just 4% of a competitor when it could not afford to update its own products?

That was why, soon after I arrived, we started dismantling our keiretsu investments. Despite widespread fears that the sell-offs would damage our relationships with suppliers, those relationships are stronger than ever. It turns out that our partners make a clear distinction between Nissan as customer and Nissan as shareholder. They don't care what we do with the shares as long as we're still a customer. In fact, they seem to have benefited from our divestments. They have not only delivered the price reductions that Nissan has demanded but also have improved their profitability. Indeed, all Nissan's suppliers posted increased profits in 2000. Although breaking up the Nissan keiretsu seemed a radical move at the time, many other Japanese companies are now following our lead.

Nissan's problems weren't just financial, however. Far from it. Our most fundamental challenge was cultural. Like other Japanese companies, Nissan paid and promoted its employees based on their tenure and age. The longer employees stuck around, the more power and money they received, regardless of their actual performance. Inevitably, that practice bred a certain degree of complacency, which undermined Nissan's competitiveness. What car buyers want, after all, is performance, performance, performance. They want well-designed, high-quality products at attractive prices, delivered on time. They don't care how the company does that or who in the company does it. It's only logical, then, to build a company's reward and incentive systems around performance, irrespective of age, gender, or nationality.

So we decided to ditch the seniority rule. Of course, that didn't mean we systematically started selecting the youngest candidates for promotion. In fact, the senior vice presidents that I've nominated over the past two years all have had long records of service, though they were usually not the most senior candidates. We looked at people's performance records, and if the highest performer was also the most senior, fine. But if the second or third or even the fifth most senior had the best track record, we did not hesitate to pass over those with longer service. As expected when changing long-standing practices, we've had some problems. When you nominate a younger person to a job in Japan, for example, he sometimes suffers for being younger—in some cases, older people may not be willing to cooperate with him as fully as they might. Of course, it's also true that an experience like that can be a good test of the quality of leadership a manager brings to the job.

We also revamped our compensation system to put the focus on performance. In the traditional Japanese compensation system, managers receive no share options, and hardly any incentives are built into the manager's pay packet. If a company's average pay raise is, say, 4%, then good performers can expect a 5% or 6% raise, and poor performers get 2% or 2.5%. The system extends to the upper reaches of management, which means that the people whose decisions have the greatest impact on the company have little incentive to get them right. We changed all that. High performers today can expect cash incentives that amount to more than a third of their annual pay packages, on top of which employees receive company stock options. Here, too, other Japanese companies are making similar changes.

Another deep-seated cultural problem we had to address was the organization's inability to accept responsibility. We had a culture of blame. If the company did poorly, it was always someone else's fault. Sales blamed product planning, product planning blamed engineering, and engineering blamed finance. Tokyo blamed Europe, and Europe blamed Tokyo. One of the root causes of this problem was the fact that managers usually did not have well-defined areas of responsibility.

Indeed, a whole cadre of senior managers, the Japanese "advisers" or "coordinators," had no operating responsibilities at all. The adviser, a familiar figure in foreign subsidiaries of Japanese companies, originally served as a consultant helping in the application of innovative Japanese management practices. That role, however, became redundant as familiarity with Japanese practices spread. Yet the advisers remained, doing little except undermining the authority of line managers. So at Nissan, we eliminated the position and put all our advisers into positions with direct operational responsibilities. I also redefined the roles of the other Nissan managers, as well as those of the Renault people I had brought with me. All of them now have line responsibilities, and everyone can see exactly what their contributions to Nissan are. When something goes wrong, people now take responsibility for fixing it.

Mobilizing Cross-Functional Teams

All these changes were dramatic ones. They went against the grain not only of Nissan's long-standing operating practices but also of some of the behavioral norms of Japanese society. I knew that if I had tried simply to impose the changes from the top, I would have failed. Instead, I decided to use as the centerpiece of the turnaround effort a set of cross-functional teams. I had used CFTs in my previous turnarounds and had found them a powerful tool for getting line managers to see beyond the functional or regional boundaries that define their direct responsibilities.

In my experience, executives in a company rarely reach across boundaries. Typically, engineers prefer solving problems with other engineers, salespeople like to work with fellow salespeople, and Americans feel more comfortable with other Americans. The trouble is that people working in functional or regional teams tend not to ask themselves as many hard questions as they should. By contrast, working together in cross-functional teams helps managers to think in new ways and challenge existing practices. The teams also provide a mechanism for explaining the necessity for change and for projecting difficult messages across the entire company.

Within a month of my arrival, we had put together nine CFTs. Their areas of responsibility ranged from research and development to organizational structure to product complexity. Together, they addressed all the key drivers of Nissan's performance. (See the table "Nissan's Cross-Functional Teams" for a detailed description of the teams, their areas of responsibility, and the principal changes they instigated.)

We put the teams to work on a fast track. They were given three months to review the company's operations and to come up with recommendations both for returning Nissan to profitability and for uncovering opportunities for future growth. The teams reported to Nissan's nine-member executive committee. And though the CFTs had no decision-making power—that was retained by the executive committee and myself—they had access to all aspects of the company's operations. Nothing was off limits.

The CFTs consisted of approximately ten members, all drawn from the ranks of the company's middle managers, that is, people with line responsibilities. Limiting the members to ten ensured that the teams' discussions would move forward at a reasonable pace; given the

Nissan's Cross-Functional Teams

This table lists the nine cross-functional teams that produced the Nissan Revival Plan, showing their composition and the objectives they identified.

Team	Business Development	Purchasing	Manufacturing & Logistics	Research & Development
CFT Leaders	• executive VP of overseas sales & marketing • executive VP of product planning	• executive VP of purchasing • executive VP of engineering	• executive VP of manufacturing • executive VP of product planning	• executive VP of purchasing • executive VP of engineering
CFT Pilot	• general manager of product planning	• general manager of purchasing	• deputy general manager of manufacturing	• general manager of engineering
Functions Represented	• product planning • engineering • manufacturing • sales & marketing	• purchasing • engineering • manufacturing • finance	• manufacturing • logistics • product planning • human resources	• engineering • purchasing • design
Team Review Focus	• profitable growth • new product opportunities • brand identity • product development lead time	• supplier relationships • product specifications and standards	• manufacturing efficiency and cost effectiveness	• R&D capacity
Objectives Based on Review	• launch 22 new models by 2002 • introduce a minicar model by 2002 in Japan	• cut number of suppliers in half • reduce costs by 20% over three years	• close three assembly plants in Japan • close two power-train plants in Japan • improve capacity utilization in Japan from 53% in 1999 to 82% in 2002	• move to a globally integrated organization • increase output efficiency by 20% per project

Team	Sales & Marketing	General & Administrative	Finance & Cost	Phaseout of Products & Parts Complexity Management	Organization
CFT Leaders	• executive VP of overseas sales & marketing • executive VP of domestic sales & marketing	• executive VP of finance (CFO) • senior VP of finance (DCFO)	• executive VP of finance (CFO) • senior VP of finance (DCFO)	• executive VP of domestic sales & marketing • executive VP of product planning	• executive VP of finance (CFO) • executive VP of manufacturing
CFT Pilot	• manager of overseas sales & marketing	• manager of finance	• deputy general manager of finance	• manager of product planning	• manager of human resources
Functions Represented	• sales & marketing • purchasing	• sales & marketing • manufacturing • finance • human resources	• finance • sales & marketing	• product planning • sales & marketing • manufacturing • engineering • finance • purchasing	• product planning • sales & marketing • manufacturing • engineering • finance • purchasing
Team Review Focus	• advertising structure • distribution structure • dealer organization • incentives	• fixed overhead costs	• shareholdings and other noncore assets • financial planning structure • working capital	• manufacturing efficiency and cost effectiveness	• organizational structure • employee incentive and pay packages
Objectives Based on Review	• move to a single global advertising agency • reduce SG&A costs by 20% • reduce distribution subsidiaries by 20% in Japan • close 10% of retail outlets in Japan • create prefecture business centers or common back offices	• reduce SG&A costs by 20% • reduce global head count by 21,000	• dispose of noncore assets • cut automotive debt in half to $5.8 billion net • reduce inventories	• reduce number of plants in Japan from seven to four by 2002 • reduce number of platforms in Japan from 24 to 15 by 2002 • reduce by 50% the variation in parts (due to differences in engines or destination, for example) for each model	• create a worldwide corporate headquarters • create regional management committees • empower program directors • implement performance-oriented compensation and bonus packages, including stock options

urgency of the situation, we could not afford to spend time in protracted debates. But we also recognized that a team of ten people would be too few to cover in any depth all the issues facing it. To get around that problem, each CFT formed a set of subteams, consisting of CFT members and other managers selected by the CFT. The subteams, each of which was also limited to ten members, focused on particular issues faced by the broader teams. For instance, the manufacturing team had four subteams, which reviewed capacity, productivity, fixed costs, and investments. All together, some 500 people worked in the CFTs and subteams.

To give CFTs authority within the organization, we appointed to each team two "leaders" drawn from the executive committee. These leaders served as the team sponsors, who would smooth the way for the team as it conducted its work and remove any institutional obstacles. Why two leaders rather than one? Having two such senior voices made it less likely that the team would focus its efforts too narrowly. For instance, we decided that Nobuo Okubo, Nissan's executive vice president for research and development, and Itaru Koeda, the executive vice president of purchasing, would lead the purchasing team. Their voices would balance each other, so that no single function's perspective would dominate.

But it was also important that the CFT process not look like a corporate-imposed blaming exercise. The team leaders, therefore, took a back seat in the actual operation of the CFTs and attended few of the meetings. The ten regular members of each CFT carried the real work, and one of them acted as the team's "pilot," taking responsibility for driving the agenda and discussions. The pilots were selected by the executive committee, and the leaders and pilots together selected the rest of the team. Typically, the pilots were managers who had front-line experience with Nissan's operating problems and credibility with the rank and file. I took a personal interest in their selection because it gave me a chance to have a close look at the next generation of Nissan leaders.

Setting up a clear process of this kind has helped managers to become much more aware of what they can achieve if they put their minds to the task. Take the purchasing team, which I had challenged to find ways to reduce supplier costs by 20% to bring Nissan in line with other car companies. I suggested that a third of the savings could be achieved through changes to engineering specifications, many of which were stricter at Nissan than at other companies. At first, the engineers didn't believe that anything like the amount I was looking for could be found in specification changes.

Yet by engaging in the CFT exercise, those very engineers proved themselves wrong. In fact, they have been able to deliver far more cost savings than I had expected through identifying a multitude of small changes. For example, it turned out that Nissan's quality standards for its headlamp parts were higher than its competitors, even though there was no discernible performance difference. By making a small reduction in standards for the surfaces of headlamp reflectors, Nissan was able to reduce the rejection rate for that component to zero. Another small reduction in the specification for heat resistance allowed Nissan to use less expensive materials for the lenses and inner panels of the headlamps. Together, the two changes decreased the cost of headlamps by 2.5%.

The result of the CFTs' three-month review was a detailed blueprint for the turnaround, the Nissan Revival Plan, which I released to the public in October

1999. This plan, developed by Nissan's own executives, included the major changes to Nissan's business practices that I described earlier. They also prescribed some harsh medicine in the form of plant closures and head count reductions, all in Japan. Inevitably, of course, the press focused on the way we were challenging Japanese business traditions—and on the staff cutbacks that were thought to be revolutionary in a society used to guarantees of lifetime employment. But necessary and important as these changes were, they were not the whole story.

Turning around a company in Nissan's state is a bit like Formula One racing. To take the highest-speed trajectory, you have to brake and accelerate, brake and accelerate all the time. The revival plan, therefore, was as much about future growth (accelerating) as it was about cutting costs (braking). We couldn't say, "There will be a time for cost reduction and then a time for growth"—we had to do both at once. So along with the cutbacks and closures, the plan included a number of major investment commitments, such as a $300 million investment to produce Nissan models at Renault's plant in Brazil and a $930 million investment for a new plant in Canton, Mississippi. We also announced our entry into the minicar market in Japan and took back control of our operations in Indonesia. (For a summary of the revival plan and our performance against it, see the exhibit "What the Numbers Show.")

The CFTs have remained an integral part of Nissan's management structure. I still meet with the pilots at least once a month, and at least once a year, I receive briefings from the full teams. We have even added a tenth team covering investment costs and efficiency. The teams' mission today is twofold. First, they serve as

What the Numbers Show

This table shows how successful the turnaround has been along the key performance dimensions laid out in the Nissan Revival Plan. The company's objectives under the plan are marked in bold: to return Nissan to profitability by 2000, to increase the operating margin to more than 4.5% by 2002, and to reduce debt to below $5.8 billion by 2002.

	FY99 Results	FY00 Results	Preliminary Results of 1st Half FY01	Forecast for FY01	Revival Plan Objectives for FY02
Operating Margin	1.4%	4.75%	6.2%	5.5%	**more than 4.5%**
Operating Profit	$6.8 million	$2.4 billion	$1.6 billion	$2.9 billion	N/A
Net Profit (loss)	($5.7 billion)	**positive result of $2.8 billion**	$1.9 billion	$2.8 billion	N/A
Net Automotive Debt	$11.2 billion	$7.9 billion	$6.7 billion	less than $6.25 billion	**less than $5.8 billion**
Capacity Utilization (Japan)	53%	51.1%	75.7%	74.1%	82%
Purchasing Cost Reduction	N/A	11%	N/A	more than 18%	20%
Number of Parts Suppliers	1,145	810 (30% reduction)	750 (35% reduction)	N/A	600 (50% reduction)
Number of Employees	148,000	133,800	128,100	N/A	127,000

Note: The conversion rate used was ¥20 = $1.

watchdogs for the ongoing implementation of the revival plan. Second, they look for new ways to improve performance. In short, they are my way of making sure that Nissan stays awake and fit.

The Importance of Respect

As might be expected, given the cutbacks we made in Japan, the public was initially uneasy about the revival plan, and I took a lot of the flak as the foreigner in charge. Inside Nissan, though, people recognized that we weren't trying to take the company over but rather were attempting to restore it to its former glory. We had the trust of employees for a simple reason: We had shown them respect. Although we were making many profound changes in the way Nissan carried out its business, we were always careful to protect Nissan's identity and its dignity as a company.

That had been true even during the original negotiations between Renault and Nissan. As many people know, Renault was not Nissan's number one choice for partner. DaimlerChrysler was the preferred counterpart, which on paper was not that surprising, given its financial muscle and reputation at the time. While Nissan was negotiating with Renault, it had also been talking to DaimlerChrysler, and I myself believed that the two would probably close a deal. In the end, however, DaimlerChrysler dropped out, believing that Nissan was too risky. In the words of one Chrysler executive, bailing out Nissan would have been like putting $5 billion into a steel container and throwing it into the ocean.

With DaimlerChrysler out of the picture, Renault was Nissan's only hope for survival. The other potential suitor, Ford, had stepped aside long ago. Under those circumstances, you might have expected Renault to tighten its terms for dealing with Nissan. But Renault decided against exploiting its short-term bargaining advantage. We took the view that we were entering a long-term relationship. If we were to start by abusing our partner, we'd pay for it later. I believe that Renault's decision to stick to the terms it had offered Nissan before Daimler-Chrysler dropped out contributed greatly to preserving the morale of Nissan managers at the start.

Since then, of course, cooperation between the two companies has dissipated all fears of foreign domination. Although the needs of the turnaround meant that Nissan was at first more of a learner than Renault, the relationship between the two companies has become evenly balanced. Renault people are now coming to learn from Nissan, and Nissan senior managers are transferring their skills to Renault business units. Indeed, after just three years with Nissan, I doubt anyone would say that the people I brought with me still belong to Renault. They have probably contributed a lot more to Nissan than to Renault. What's more, it sometimes seems to me that as Nissan's identity strengthens, the North Americans, Europeans, and Japanese working here are becoming much more alike than they are different.

On the whole, I think Nissan's identity and culture as a company have been far more important factors in its performance than its country of origin, and I think this would be true for most companies. In fact, looking to national culture for an explanation of a company's failure or success almost always means you are missing the point. All that a national culture does is provide the company with the raw human resources for competing. Obviously, if those resources are untrained or the business environment is undeveloped, even the best company can do little. But equally, no matter how promising your resources, you will never be able to turn them into gold unless you get the corporate culture right. A good corporate culture taps into the productive aspects of a country's culture, and in Nissan's case we have been able to exploit the uniquely Japanese combination of keen competitiveness and sense of community that has driven the likes of Sony and Toyota—and Nissan itself in earlier times.

Building Trust Through Transparency

FOR A TURNAROUND PROCESS of this kind to work, people have to believe both that they can speak the truth and that they can trust what they hear from others. Building trust, however, is a long-term project; those in charge have to demonstrate that they do what they say they'll do, and that takes time. But you have to start somewhere. Right from the beginning, I made it clear that every number had to be thoroughly checked. I did not accept any report that was less than totally clear and verifiable, and I expected people to personally commit to every observation or claim they made. I set the example myself; when I announced the revival plan, I also declared that I would resign if we failed to accomplish any of the commitments we set for ourselves.

On a broader level, I also sought to impose transparency on the entire organization to ensure that everyone knew what everyone else was doing. Traditionally, for example, the company's European and North American units operated independently, sharing little information and expertise with the rest of the company. Each unit had its own president and regional team, who were supposed to build links to corporate headquarters and thus to the rest of the corporation. In reality, however, the regional presidents and their teams were building walls, and there was little cooperation between different parts of the company.

I decided, therefore, to do away with the post of regional president and announced the change in March 2000, six months after the publication of Nissan's overall revival plan. Today, four management committees, meeting once a month, supervise Nissan's regional operations. Each committee includes representatives of the major functions: manufacturing, purchasing, sales and marketing, finance, and so on. I chair the committee for Japan, while the committees supervising the European, U.S., and general overseas markets are chaired by Nissan executive vice presidents based in Japan. I also make sure that I attend the European and North American committee meetings at least four times a year. This reorganization was one of the few changes I made unilaterally, but it was consistent with my commitment to transparency inside the organization.

From Cross-Function to Cross-Company

CROSS-FUNCTIONAL TEAMWORK has been central to the Nissan turnaround. A similar approach has also emerged as a key element behind the success of the Nissan-Renault alliance.

At a certain point in negotiations between the two companies, there was a discussion about how they would work together. Renault's negotiators assumed that the best way forward would be to set up a series of joint ventures, and they wanted to discuss all legal issues surrounding a joint venture: who contributes what and how much, how the output is shared, and so forth. The Nissan team pushed back; they wanted to explore management and business issues, not legal technicalities. As a result, negotiations were stalled.

Renault CEO Louis Schweitzer asked me if I could think of a way to resolve that impasse. I recommended abandoning the joint-venture approach. If you want people to work together, the last thing you need is a legal structure that gets in the way. My solution was to introduce informal cross-company teams (CCTs). Some teams focused on specific aspects of automobile manufacturing and delivery—there was a team focusing on product planning, for instance, and another on manufacturing and logistics. Others focused on a region—Europe, for instance, and Mexico and Central America. All told, we created 11 such cross-company teams.

Through these teams, Renault and Nissan managers have found many ways to leverage the strengths of both companies. The experience of the Mexico regional CCT is a good example. At the time of the alliance in early 1999, Nissan was suffering from overcapacity in the Mexican market because of sluggish domestic demand and flagging sales of the aging Sentra model to the United States. Renault, on the other hand, was thinking about reentering the Mexican market, which it had abandoned in 1986. Putting managers from both companies together meant that they immediately recognized the synergy opportunity. In just five months, they put together a detailed plan for producing Renault cars in Nissan's plants. Just over a year later, in December 2000, the first Renault models rolled off the production lines.

The improvement in Nissan's manufacturing position has been dramatic. At the Cuernavaca plant, the capacity utilization rate has risen from 55% at the end of 1998 to nearly 100%. For Renault's part, the arrangement greatly accelerated its reentry into Mexico. In fact, Renault was able to begin selling cars in Mexico even before the first Scenic rolled off the production line. Because the Mexican government recognized Renault as a partner of the Nissan group, Renault was able to immediately export cars to Mexico without having to obtain separate government approval. What's more, Renault could use Nissan's local dealers as distributors.

Today the cross-country teams and the cross-functional teams have complementary roles: The company CFTs serve as guardians of each company's revival plan, while the CCTs feed the alliance.

Originally published in January 2002
Reprint R0201B

When Is Virtual Virtuous?
Organizing for Innovation

HENRY W. CHESBROUGH AND
DAVID J. TEECE

Executive Summary

CHAMPIONS OF VIRTUAL CORPORATIONS are urging
managers to subcontract anything and everything.
Because a number of high-profile corporate giants have
been outperformed by more nimble, "networked"
competitors, the idea of the virtual organization is tantalizing. But is virtual really the best way to organize for
innovation?

Henry W. Chesbrough and David J. Teece argue
that the virtual corporation has been oversold. Innovation
is not monolithic, and it is critically important to understand the type of innovation in question. For some innovations, joint ventures, alliances, and outsourcing can play
a useful role. But for others, they are inappropriate—and
strategically dangerous. The initial success—and subsequent failure—of the IBM PC illustrate the strategic

mistake of using a virtual approach for the kind of complex technology that should have been controlled in-house.

The authors present a framework to help managers determine when to innovate by going virtual, when to form alliances, and when to rely on internal development. They provide a range of cases to illustrate how to match organizational strategy to the type of innovation being pursued. General Motors, for example, used the wrong approach to develop disc brake technology and paid the price: getting to market later than its competitors. To realize its vision of "tetherless communication," Motorola must choose an organizational strategy allowing it more control over the directions and timing of technological change than a virtual approach could provide. In contrast, the virtues of the virtual organization are illustrated by Ameritech's use of alliances to influence the innovation path in multimedia.

CHAMPIONS OF VIRTUAL CORPORATIONS are urging managers to subcontract anything and everything. All over the world, companies are jumping on the bandwagon, decentralizing, downsizing, and forging alliances to pursue innovation. Why is the idea of the virtual organization so tantalizing? Because we have come to believe that bureaucracy is bad and flexibility is good. And so it follows that a company that invests in as little as possible will be more responsive to a changing marketplace and more likely to attain global competitive advantage.

There is no question that many large and cumbersome organizations have been outperformed by smaller "networked" competitors. Consider the eclipse of IBM in

PCs and of DEC in workstations by Packard Bell and Sun Microsystems. But while there are many successful virtual companies, there are even more failures that don't make the headlines. After many years of studying the relationship between organization and innovation, we believe that the virtues of being virtual have been oversold. The new conventional wisdom ignores the distinctive role that large integrated companies can play in the innovation process. Those rushing to form alliances instead of nurturing and guarding their own capabilities may be risking their future.

What's Special About Virtual?

What gives the virtual company its advantage? In essence, incentives and responsiveness. Virtual companies coordinate much of their business through the marketplace, where free agents come together to buy and sell one another's goods and services; thus virtual companies can harness the power of

The incentives that make a virtual company powerful also leave it vulnerable.

market forces to develop, manufacture, market, distribute, and support their offerings in ways that fully integrated companies can't duplicate. As William Joy, vice president of research and development at Sun Microsystems, puts it, "Not all the smart people [in the workstation industry] work for Sun." Because an outside developer of workstation software can obtain greater rewards by selling software to Sun customers than by developing the same software as a Sun employee, he or she will move faster, work harder, and take more risks. Using high-powered, market-based incentives such as stock options and attractive bonuses, a virtual company

can quickly access the technical resources it needs, if those resources are available. In situations where technology is changing rapidly, large companies that attempt to do everything inside will flounder when competing against small companies with highly trained and motivated employees.

But the incentives that make a virtual company powerful also leave it vulnerable. As incentives become greater and risk taking increases, coordination among parties through the marketplace becomes more and more difficult, precisely because so much personal reward is at stake. Each party to joint development activity necessarily acts in its own self-interest. Over time, innovation can generate unforeseen surprises that work to the advantage of some parties and to the disadvantage of others. The result: Once-friendly partners may be unwilling or unable to align strategically, and coordinated development activity falters. In contrast, integrated, centralized companies do not generally reward people for taking risks, but they do have established processes for settling conflicts and coordinating all the activities necessary for innovation.

This trade-off between incentives and control lies at the heart of the decision that managers must make about how to organize for innovation. (See the graph "Finding the Right Degree of Centralization.") If virtual organizations and integrated companies are at opposite ends of the spectrum, alliances occupy a kind of organizational middle ground. An alliance can achieve some of the coordination of an integrated company, but, like players in a virtual network, the members of an alliance will be driven to enhance their own positions, and over time their interests may diverge. The challenge for managers is to choose the organizational form that best matches the type of innovation they are pursuing.

Types of Innovation

When should companies organize for innovation by using decentralized (or virtual) approaches, and when should they rely on internal organization? The answer depends on the innovation in question.

Some innovations are *autonomous*—that is, they can be pursued independently from other innovations. A new turbocharger to increase horsepower in an automobile engine, for example, can be developed without a complete redesign of the engine or the rest of the car. In contrast, some innovations are fundamentally *systemic*—that is, their benefits can be realized only in conjunction with related, complementary innovations. To profit from instant photography, Polaroid needed to develop both new film technology and new camera

Finding the Right Degree of Centralization

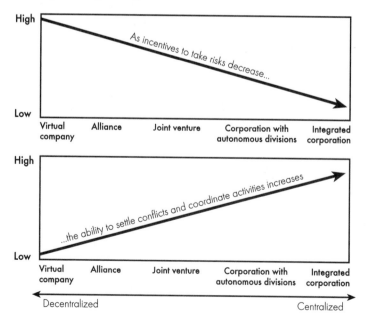

technology. Similarly, lean manufacturing is a systemic innovation because it requires interrelated changes in product design, supplier management, information technology, and so on.

The distinction between autonomous and systemic innovation is fundamental to the choice of organizational design. When innovation is autonomous, the decentralized virtual organization can manage the development and commercialization tasks quite well. When innovation is systemic, members of a virtual organization are dependent on the other members, over whom they have no control. In either case, the wrong organizational choice can be costly.

Consider what happened to General Motors when the automobile industry shifted from drum brakes to disc brakes, an autonomous innovation. General Motors was slow to adopt disc brakes because it had integrated vertically in the production of the old technology. GM's more decentralized competitors relied instead on market relationships with their suppliers—and the high-powered incentives inherent in those relationships. As a result, they were able to beat GM to market with the new disc brakes, which car buyers wanted. When companies inappropriately use centralized approaches to manage autonomous innovations, as GM did in this case, small companies and more decentralized large companies will usually outperform them.

To understand why the two types of innovation call for different organizational strategies, consider the information flow essential to innovation. Information about new products and technologies often develops over time as managers absorb new research findings, the results of early product experiments, and initial customer feedback. To commercialize an innovation profitably, a

tremendous amount of knowledge from industry players, from customers, and sometimes from scientists must be gathered and understood. This task is easier if the information is codified.

Codified information—for example, specifications that are captured in industry standards and design rules—can often be transferred almost as effectively from one company to another as it can within a single company. Because such information is easily duplicated, it has little natural protection. Sometimes bits and pieces can be protected by intellectual property rights, but those pieces, especially trade secrets and patents, are small islands in a broad ocean of knowledge.

Other information does not travel as easily between companies. Tacit knowledge is knowledge that is implicitly grasped or used but has not been fully articulated, such as the know-how of a master craftsman or the ingrained perspectives of a specific company or work unit. Because such knowledge is deeply embedded in individuals or companies, it tends to diffuse slowly and only with effort and the transfer of people. Established companies can protect the tacit knowledge they hold, sharing only codified information. They can be quite strategic about what they disclose and when they disclose it.

The information needed to integrate an autonomous innovation with existing technologies is usually well understood and may even be codified in industry standards. Systemic innovations, on the other hand, pose a unique set of management challenges regarding information exchange. By their very nature, systemic innovations require information sharing and coordinated adjustment *throughout an entire product system.* Here is where a market-based, virtual approach to innovation poses serious strategic hazards. Unaffiliated companies linked through arm's-length contracts often cannot achieve sufficient coordination. Each company wants the other to do more, while each is also looking for ways to realize the most gain from the innovation. Information sharing can be reduced or biased, as each seeks to get the most at the other's expense. In most cases, the open exchange of information that fuels systemic innovation will be easier and safer within a company than across company boundaries. The inevitable conflicts and choices that arise as a systemic innovation develops can best be resolved by an integrated company's internal management processes.

The Case of Industry Standards

Coordinating a systemic innovation is particularly difficult when industry standards do not exist and must be pioneered. In such instances, virtual organizations are likely to run into strategic problems. Consider how technical standards emerge. Market participants weigh many competing technologies and eventually rally around one of them. There are winners and losers among the contestants, and potential losers can try to undermine the front-runner or to fragment the standard by promoting a rival. Until a clear winner emerges, customers may choose to sit on the sidelines rather than risk making the wrong choice.

By virtue of its size and scope, an integrated company may be able to advance a new standard simply by choosing to adopt a particular technology. If a large company commits itself to one of a host of competing technologies, consumers as well as companies promoting rival technologies will probably be persuaded to follow suit.

Virtual companies, however, which may be struggling to resolve conflicts within their networks, won't be able to break a deadlock in a complicated standards battle. Players in a network won't be able to coordinate themselves to act like a large company.

Once a new standard has been established, virtual organizations can manage further innovation quite well. But when an industry begins to advance technology to a new level, the cycle can begin anew. Again, technically feasible choices present new strategic trade-offs. Suppliers, competitors, and customers may fail to agree on a common path. Unless a big player emerges to break the logjam among rival technologies, the existing standard will prevail long past its usefulness.

Today computer floppy disks are frozen in an old standard because no single company has been able to establish a new one. IBM pioneered the 3.5-inch hardcase diskette in 1987 when it introduced its new line of PS/2 personal computers. Within two years, the memory capacity of 3.5-inch diskettes doubled from 720 kilobytes to 1.44 megabytes, where it has remained ever since.

Why? The technical capability to expand diskette capacity is available, but no company has the reputation and strength to set a new standard. Through the 1980s, IBM was large enough to coordinate standards among the key participants in the industry: personal computer manufacturers, diskette makers, and software publishers. If IBM told the industry it would use a particular capacity on its next generation of machines, others did the same. But in the 1990s, IBM's leadership of the PC market came to an end, perhaps permanently. Today IBM is not strong enough to move the industry by itself, and it won't move ahead of the other industry players and risk being stranded if they don't follow.

A simple rule of thumb applies: When innovation depends on a series of interdependent innovations—that is, when innovation is systemic—independent companies will not usually be able to coordinate themselves to knit those innovations together. Scale, integration, and market leadership may be required to establish and then to advance standards in an industry.

The IBM PC: Virtual Success or Failure?

IBM's development of the personal computer is a fascinating example of both the advantages and disadvantages of using virtual approaches to pursue innovation. When IBM launched its first PC in 1981, the company elected to outsource all the major components from the marketplace. By tapping the capabilities of other companies, IBM was able to get its first product to market in only 15 months. The

More than a few analysts hailed IBM's development of the PC as a new business model.

microprocessor (the 8088) was purchased from Intel, and the operating system (which became PC-DOS) was licensed from a then fledgling software company, Microsoft. In effect, the IBM PC had an "open" architecture: It was based on standards and components that were widely available. The high-powered incentives of the marketplace could coordinate the roles of component manufacturers and software vendors. IBM successfully promoted its open architecture to hundreds of third-party developers of software applications and hardware accessory products, knowing that those products would add to the appeal of the PC.

IBM also relied on the market to distribute the product. Although IBM launched its own IBM Product Centers as retail storefronts and had its own direct sales force for large corporate customers, the majority of the company's systems were distributed through independent retailers, initially ComputerLand and Sears. Eventually, there were more than 2,000 retail outlets.

By using outside parties for hardware, software, and distribution, IBM greatly reduced its investment in bringing the PC to market. More important, those relationships allowed IBM to launch an attack against Apple, which had pioneered the market and was growing quickly. The IBM PC was an early success, and it spawned what became the dominant architecture of the entire microcomputer industry. By 1984, three years after the introduction of the PC, IBM replaced Apple as the number one supplier of microcomputers, with 26% of the PC business. By 1985, IBM's share had grown to 41%. Many observers attributed the PC's success to IBM's creative use of outside relationships. More than a few business analysts hailed the IBM PC development as a model for doing business in the future.

Indeed, IBM's approach in its PC business is exactly the kind of decentralized strategy that commentators are urging large, slow-moving companies to adopt. The early years of the IBM PC show many of the benefits of using markets and outside companies to coordinate innovation: fast development of technology and tremendous technological improvements from a wide variety of sources.

With the passage of time, though, the downside of IBM's decentralized approach has become apparent. IBM failed to anticipate that its virtual and open approach would prevent the company from directing the PC architecture it had created. The open architecture and the autonomy of its vendors invited design mutinies and the entry of IBM-compatible PC manufacturers. At first, competitors struggled to achieve compatibility with IBM's architecture, but after several years compatibility was widespread in the industry. And once that happened, manufacturers could purchase the same CPU from Intel and the same operating system from Microsoft, run the same application software (from Lotus, Microsoft, WordPerfect, and others), and sell through the same distribution channels (such as ComputerLand, BusinessLand, and MicroAge). IBM had little left on which to establish a competitive advantage.

To maintain technological leadership, IBM decided to advance the PC architecture. To do that, IBM needed to coordinate the many interrelated pieces of the architecture—a systemic technology coordination task. However, the third-party hardware and software suppliers that had helped establish the original architecture did not follow IBM's lead. When IBM introduced its OS/2 operating system, the company could not stop Microsoft from introducing Windows, an application that works with the old DOS operating system, thereby greatly reducing the advantages of switching to OS/2. And third-party hardware and software companies made investments that extended the usefulness of the original PC architecture. Similarly, Intel helped Compaq steal a march on IBM in 1986, when Compaq introduced the first PC based on Intel's 80386 microprocessor, an enhancement over the earlier generations of microprocessors used in IBM and compatible machines. Even though IBM owned 12% of Intel at the time, it couldn't prevent Intel from working with Compaq to beat IBM to market. This was the beginning of the end of IBM's ability to direct the evolution of PC architecture.

By the third quarter of 1995, IBM's share of the PC market had fallen to just 7.3%, trailing Compaq's 10.5% share. Today its PC business is rumored to be modestly profitable at best. Most of the profits from the PC architecture have migrated upstream to the supplier of the microprocessor (Intel) and the operating system (Microsoft), and to outside makers of application software. The combined market value of those suppliers and third parties today greatly exceeds IBM's.

IBM's experience in the PC market illustrates the strategic importance of organization in the pursuit of innovation. Virtual approaches encounter serious problems when companies seek to exploit systemic innovation. Key development activities that depend on one another must be conducted in-house to capture the rewards from long-term R&D investments. Without directed coordination, the necessary complementary innovations required to leverage a new technology may not be forthcoming.

The Virtuous Virtuals

How have the most successful virtual companies accomplished the difficult task of coordination? The virtual companies that have demonstrated staying power are all at the center of a network that they use to leverage their own capabilities. Few virtual companies that have survived and prospered have outsourced everything. Rather, the virtuous virtuals have carefully nurtured and guarded the internal capabilities that provide the essential underpinnings of competitive advantage. And they invest considerable resources to maintain and extend their core competencies internally. Indeed, without these companies' unique competencies and capabilities, their strategic position in the network would be short-lived.

Consider the well-known battle between MIPS Technologies and Sun Microsystems for control of workstation processors. (See Benjamin Gomes-Casseres, "Group Versus Group: How Alliance Networks Compete," Chapter 4.) MIPS was trying to promote its Advanced Computing Environment (ACE) against Sun's Scalable Processor Architecture (SPARC). Sun had strong internal capabilities, whereas MIPS tried to compete as a more virtual player, leveraging off of the competencies of partners such as Compaq, DEC, and Silicon Graphics. MIPS had a good technical design, but that was literally all it had, and this hollowness left the company at the mercy of its partners. As soon as DEC and Compaq reduced their commitment to the ACE initiative, the network fell apart and pulled MIPS down with it. The very reliance of virtual companies on partners, suppliers, and other outside companies exposes them to strategic hazards. Put another way, there are plenty of small, dynamic companies that have not been able to outperform larger competitors. In particular, a hollow company like MIPS is ill equipped to coordinate a network of companies. Although Sun also worked with alliance partners, it had strong internal capabilities in systems design, manufacturing, marketing, sales, service, and support. As a result, Sun can direct and advance the SPARC architecture, a dominant technology in the industry.

Many companies with superior capabilities have prospered as the dominant player in a network. Japanese keiretsu are structured that way. Consider Toyota, whose successful introduction of the lean production system—a truly systemic innovation—required tremendous coordination with its network of suppliers. Because Toyota was much larger than its suppliers, and because, until recently, it was the largest customer of virtually all of them, it could compel those suppliers to make radical changes in their business practices. In a more egalitarian network, suppliers can demand a large share of the economic benefits of innovations, using what economists call hold-up strategies. Strong central players like Toyota are rarely vulnerable to such tactics and are thus in a better position to drive and coordinate systemic innovation.

The most successful virtual companies sit at the center of networks that are far from egalitarian. Nike may rely on Asian partners for manufacturing, but its capabilities in design and marketing allow it to call all the shots. In the computer industry, Intel has effective control of the 80X86 microprocessor standard, Microsoft dominates PC operating systems, and Sun is driving the SPARC architecture. Those companies control and coordinate the advance of technologies in their areas, and in this regard they function more like integrated companies than like market-based virtuals.

Choosing the Right Organizational Design

Today few companies can afford to develop internally all the technologies that might provide an advantage in the future. In every company we studied, we found a mix of approaches: Some technologies were "purchased" from other companies; others were acquired through licenses, partnerships, and alliances; and still other critical technologies were developed internally. Getting the right balance is crucial, as IBM's disastrous experience in PCs illustrates. But what constitutes the right balance?

Consider how a successful innovator such as Motorola evaluates the trade-offs. Motorola, a leader in wireless communications technology, has declared its long-term goal to be the delivery of "untethered communication"—namely, communication anytime, anywhere, without the need for wires, power cords, or other constraints. In order to achieve that goal, Motorola must make important decisions about where and how to advance the required technologies. Those decisions turn on a handful of questions: Is the technology systemic or likely to become systemic in the future? What capabilities exist in-house and in the current supplier base? When will needed technologies become available?

For Motorola, battery technology is critical because it determines the functionality that can be built into a handheld communications device and the length of time that the device can be used before recharging. Batteries have been a pacing technology in this area for many years.

As Motorola scans the horizon for improved battery technology, it encounters a familiar trade-off between the degree of technological advancement and the number of reliable volume suppliers. Conventional battery technologies such as nickel cadmium (Ni-Cd) have become commodities, and there are many suppliers. But few if any suppliers can offer the more advanced technologies Motorola needs. And the most exotic technologies, such as fuel cells and solid-state energy sources, are not yet commercially viable from any supplier. How should Motorola organize to obtain each of the technologies it might need? Under what circumstances should the company buy the technology from a supplier and when should it form alliances or joint ventures? When should Motorola commit to internal development of the technology? (See the matrix "Matching Organization to Innovation.")

For Ni-Cd technology, the clear choice for Motorola is to buy the technology, or to use the market to coordinate access to this technology, because Motorola can rely on competition among many qualified suppliers to deliver what it wants, when needed, for a competitive price. Motorola faces a more complex decision for fuel cells and solid-state battery technologies. Should Motorola wait until those technologies are more widely available, or should the company opt for a joint venture or internal development?

Before deciding to wait for cutting-edge battery technologies to be developed, Motorola must consider three

Matching Organization to Innovation

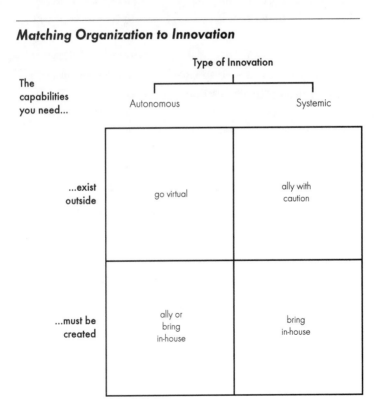

issues. One is that Motorola could lose the ability to influence the direction of the technology; the early commercial forms may be designed for applications that do not benefit Motorola, such as electric automobiles. The second problem is that Motorola might lose the ability to pace the technology, to bring it to market at a competitively desirable time. The third issue is that if such technologies are—or become—systemic and Motorola has no control over them, the company may not be able to advance related technologies and design features to achieve its goal of untethered communication.

Those issues suggest that Motorola cannot simply wait for the technologies to be provided by the market. Rather, Motorola needs to build strong ties to suppliers with the best capabilities, thus increasing its ability to direct the path of future systemic innovation. Where Motorola itself has strong capabilities, the company should pursue the technologies on its own.

To retain its leadership over the long term, Motorola must continue to develop the critical parts of its value chain internally and acquire less critical technologies from the market or from alliances. Although networks with their high-powered incentives may be effective over the short term for an unchanging technology, they will not adapt well over the long term as technology develops and companies must depend on certain internal capabilities to keep up. The popularity of networked companies and decentralization arises, in part, from observations over a time horizon that is far too short. Remember the enthusiasm that greeted IBM's early success in PCs.

Scale and Scope

Business history presents us with a lesson of striking relevance to the organizational decisions managers face today. In the classic *Scale and Scope*, Alfred Chandler details how the modern corporation evolved in the United States, Germany, and Great Britain at the end of the nineteenth century. Managers who invested the capital to build large-scale enterprises blazed the trail for the leading industries of the second industrial revolution. Markets in railroads, steel, chemicals, and petroleum were developed and shaped by major companies, not the other way around. The most successful of those companies were the first in their industries to make the massive investments in manufacturing, management, and distribution that were needed to realize the gains from innovation.

Companies that failed to make such coordinated, internal commitments during this period were soon thrust aside. The experience of British companies provides a cautionary tale for the champions of the virtual company. Many enjoyed early technological leads in their industries, but the reluctance of those family-run companies to relinquish control to outside investors prevented them from investing to build the capabilities they needed to commercialize their technologies. When German or U.S. competitors made the requisite investments, British companies lost their leadership position. In chemicals, for example, the British lead in the 1870s was completely lost by 1890. History even provided British chemical companies with a second chance when Germany's defeat in World War I temporarily cost German chemical manufacturers their plants and distribution networks. But by 1930, German chemical companies regained the lead because the British again failed to invest adequately. The lesson is that companies that develop their own capabilities can outperform those that rely too heavily on coordination through markets and alliances to build their businesses.

The leading industries of the late nineteenth and early twentieth centuries—chemicals, steel, and railroads—all experienced rapid systemic innovation. The winners were the companies that made major internal investments to shape the markets, rather than those that relied on others to lead the way. While business conditions have certainly changed, many of the principles that worked a century ago still pertain.

Today leading companies like Intel and Microsoft make extensive investments to enhance their current capabilities and spur the creation of new ones. Because so many important innovations are systemic, decentralization without strategic leverage and coordination is exactly the wrong organizational strategy. In most cases, only a large company will have the scale and scope to coordinate complementary innovations. For both the chemicals industry 100 years ago and the microcomputer industry today, long-term success requires considerable and sustained internal investment within a company. The lessons of the second industrial revolution apply to the third: Adept, well-managed companies that commit the right internal resources to innovation will shape the markets and build the new industries of the twenty-first century.

Ameritech's Strategy for Emerging Technologies

AMERITECH, A REGIONAL BELL Operating Company with wire and fiber assets in the Midwest, has the potential to be a major player in the development of on-demand video and interactive information services for home use. In emerging technologies such as multimedia, no one has all the information to determine what capabilities a company must develop internally or access through the market. The only certainty is that the promise of this market will depend on the co-development of many technologies, including data formats, throughput rates, wiring topologies, billing systems, and user interfaces.

Because the eventual configuration of the multimedia industry is unknown (and arguably unknowable ex ante), organizations such as Ameritech must become insiders to the discussions among a range of potential industry players. In emerging markets that are dependent on evolving technologies, considerable information sharing among a wide variety of companies will ultimately result in a road map for the industry. Virtual organizations can serve as catalysts to the development of industry directions and standards in ways that fully integrated organizations cannot.

Consider the role of alliances in Ameritech's multimedia strategy. By allying its own capabilities with those of companies with relevant and complementary skills, Ameritech can participate directly in defining and developing an architecture that will ultimately manage the emerging technologies. One such alliance is with Random House, a leading print publisher of books and magazines, with properties such as the *New Yorker*, Condé Nast, Fodor's, and Arthur Frommer Travel Guides. Random House is capable of supplying significant "content" over Ameritech's wires into the home. This alliance allows both companies to begin to explore the business and technical requirements of providing content into the home.

Ameritech and Random House have formed a joint venture to acquire a start-up virtual company called

Worldview Systems, which publishes an electronic monthly current-events database of travel information about more than 170 destinations around the world. While Worldview Systems' products are now sold primarily through travel agents and an 800 telephone number, Ameritech and Random House believe that this type of product may turn out to be ideal for delivery to the home. As Thomas Touton, Ameritech Development's vice president for venture capital, notes, such exploratory investments "require support from senior management willing to move fast in investing but be patient in waiting for returns, and an investment focus that is strongly synergistic with the company's operations."

When and if the promise of the multimedia market becomes real, Ameritech will doubtless be competing against other powerful players. But Ameritech may already have an inside track in the race to deliver information and video on demand into the home. Through alliances such as the one with Random House and exploratory investments in virtual companies such as Worldview Systems, Ameritech has been able to share information and know-how with other potential industry participants and become an insider with the potential to influence the direction of this nascent industry. Until a technological direction becomes clear, companies must invest in capabilities and become active participants in the information dissemination process. Virtual organizations can be an extremely valuable tool at this early stage of market evolution.

Originally published in January–February 1996
Reprint 96103

The Way to Win in Cross-Border Alliances

JOEL BLEEKE AND DAVID ERNST

Executive Summary

WAR STORIES ABOUT FAILED ALLIANCES make executives wary of forging new joint ventures and unsure about how to manage the ones they have. But the strategic benefits of cross-border alliances are compelling, and there is a wealth of experience to learn from. In fact, a study of 49 cross-border alliances of the top U.S., Japanese, and European companies found several patterns that have managerial implications.

The study found, for instance, that unlike cross-border acquisitions, cross-border alliances are most suitable for edging into new businesses or for expanding existing businesses into new geographic regions. It also found that alliances formed to buttress a weak company generally don't succeed. One joint venture to manufacture cars in Europe failed despite the many strengths of the Japanese partner. The European partner, which was supposed to provide the management skill, was simply too weak and dragged down the whole venture. Alliances must be free to evolve as the environment changes and opportunities arise. That explains why alliances like the ones between Toshiba and Motorola, GE and Snecma, and Corning and Siemens have been so successful and long lasting. Contrary to conventional wisdom, fifty-fifty ownership of joint ventures improves decision making, and most alliance end with one parent acquiring the venture.

IN THE FACE OF NEWLY opening markets, intensified competition, and the need for increased scale, many CEOs have put the formation of cross-border alliances on their agendas for the 1990s. To international managers, the strategic benefits are compelling: alliances are an expedient way to crack new markets, to gain skills, technology, or products, and to share fixed costs and resources. Yet a lot of the war stories suggest that alliances are all but doomed to failure, and CEOs setting up cross-border alliances or dealing with early problems find little is systematically known about how to make alliances succeed.

To better understand cross-border alliances and what it takes to make them work, we examined the partnerships of 150 top companies ranked by market value (50 each from the United States, Europe, and Japan). The 49 strategic alliances that we studied in detail varied widely in size, location, industry, and structure. Some were established to speed entry into a new market, others to develop and commercialize new products; still others to gain skills or share costs.

Our analysis found that although cross-border alliances pose many challenges, they are in fact viable vehicles for international strategy. While two-thirds of cross-border alliances run into serious managerial or financial trouble within the first two years, many overcome their problems. Of the 49 we analyzed, 51% were successful for both partners. Only 33% resulted in failure for both.

How can managers maximize their chances of success in these ventures? What wisdom can be derived from the experiences to date? Here are a few of our findings:

- Arguments over whether cross-border alliances or cross-border acquisitions are superior are beside the point; both have roughly a 50% rate of success. But acquisitions work well for core businesses and existing geographic areas, while alliances are more effective for edging into related businesses or new geographic markets.

- Alliances between strong and weak companies rarely work. They do not provide the missing skills needed for growth, and they lead to mediocre performance.

- The hallmark of successful alliances that endure is their ability to evolve beyond initial expectations and objectives. This requires autonomy for the venture and flexibility on the part of the parents.

- Alliances with an even split of financial ownership are more likely to succeed than those in which one partner holds a majority interest. What matters is clear management control, not financial ownership.

- More than 75% of the alliances that terminated ended with an acquisition by one of the parents.

All of these findings have implications for creating and managing successful cross-border alliances.

Related Businesses, New Geographic Markets

Both cross-border alliances and cross-border acquisitions are good vehicles for international strategy and have similar success rates (51% and 57% respectively). But that doesn't mean they are interchangeable. When used to expand core businesses, both cross-border alliances and acquisitions work well. But for expanding existing businesses into new geographic regions or for edging out into new businesses, cross-border alliances work better.

The Crédit Suisse-First Boston alliance worked because each parent had a market presence.

When moving into new geographic markets, managers should try to structure alliances to capitalize on the distinctive geographic positions of the partners. Some 62% of the alliances that involved partners with different geographic strengths succeeded (see the exhibit, "Does Geographic Overlap Help or Hinder Cross-Border Alliances?"). This is very different from the finding for cross-border acquisitions: the success rate was just 8% when the acquirer and the target company did not have significant overlapping presences in the same geographic markets.

Crédit Suisse-First Boston, a joint venture formed in 1978 to expand both companies' positions in the Eurobond market, shows the benefits of using alliances to leverage complementary geographic strengths. First Boston provided access to U.S. corporate issuers of

Does Geographic Overlap Help or Hinder Cross-Border Alliances?

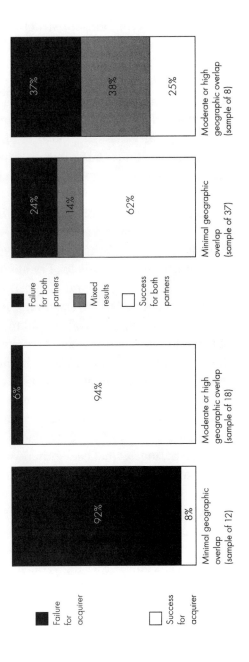

It Helps Mergers and Acquisitions...

But It Hinders Alliances

Failure for acquirer

Success for acquirer

Minimal geographic overlap (sample of 12)
- 92%
- 8%

Moderate or high geographic overlap (sample of 18)
- 6%
- 94%

Failure for both partners

Mixed results

Success for both partners

Minimal geographic overlap (sample of 37)
- 24%
- 14%
- 62%

Moderate or high geographic overlap (sample of 8)
- 37%
- 38%
- 25%

bonds and possessed the skills for structuring new financial vehicles like convertible Eurobonds. Crédit Suisse provided the capability to place issues with investors in Europe. This combination allowed the joint venture to assume a leading role in the rapidly growing Eurobond markets in the early 1980s. (The joint venture was bought out by Crédit Suisse in 1988 after First Boston began to experience financial problems, which were partly due to increasing competitiveness in the Eurobond markets.)

To build the position of core businesses in existing geographic markets, managers should use acquisitions instead of alliances. For acquisitions focused on existing markets, the success rate was 94%. For alliances in which partners had overlapping geographic positions, it was 25%. When both partners have a presence in the same geographic markets, alliances often lead to competitive conflicts. In one cross-border venture to manufacture and sell telecommunications products in the United States, one of the parents continued to sell a competing product line through a separate sales force. In theory, the two sales forces were targeting different customer segments, but because they were poorly coordinated, they ended up competing against each other. Within two years, the venture was acquired by one of the parents, and the sales forces were combined.

In the few instances in which companies have tried to use acquisitions instead of alliances to diversify abroad, they have had trouble withstanding the financial and operational strain. Not surprisingly, most companies pass up the challenge of making an acquisition to enter a new business overseas. Of the 28 cross-border acquisition programs in our study, 22 were focused on geographic expansion of core businesses; in 13 of the 16 successful programs, the acquirer already had a substantial presence in the target countries and was expanding a core business.

Managers should avoid acquisitions outside the core business, especially in new geographic markets, because they are extremely challenging and often fail. Take, for example, the British service company that acquired a Canadian electronics manufacturer to try to become a global player in the office automation industry. The Canadian company, a large second-tier player, was under intense competitive pressure: demand was soft, prices were falling, and competitors were merging to gain economies of scale. Under the new parent, the Canadian company took several steps, including rationalizing manufacturing operations to cut costs and spinning off a small subsidiary. But the U.K. company, with little direct experience in the North American market, was unable to make the needed improvements in distribution and sales, which had been weak before the merger. The new parent also had no manufacturing facilities in North America and so was unable to expand volume to drive down costs. Finally, after absorbing five years of operating losses and losing a considerable amount of senior management's time, the parent decided to divest the business at a fraction of its purchase price.

Unlike cross-border acquisitions, cross-border alliances can work well for moving into new or related businesses. Corning's well-publicized joint venture with Siemens to produce fiber-optic cable is an example of a successful move into a related business. The Siecor joint venture, started in 1977, succeeded for many reasons. For one thing, the parents brought complementary skills and capabilities. Corning had developed and patented processes to manufacture high-quality optical fibers.

Siemens had capital, scale, and worldwide distribution of telecommunications cable. Siemens also brought the manufacturing technology and equipment to produce cable from fiber. The alliance had distinct advantages over an acquisition. It allowed the creation of an enterprise focused on commercializing fiber-optic cable, and it relieved some of the financial pressure by dividing the investment. Moreover, neither company had to recoup an acquisition premium.

Equal Strength

It stands to reason that alliances between two strong partners are a safer bet than alliances between two weak partners. But many strong companies actually seek smaller or weaker companies to partner with in order to control the venture. Weaker companies often seek a strong partner to get them out of trouble or to build their skills. Our analysis suggests that these strategies do not work well because the "weak link" becomes a drag on the venture's competitiveness and causes friction between the parents. Alliances in which one partner is consistently strong in the functions it brings to the venture while the other is not strong succeeded only one-third of the time. Similarly, alliances between two financially strong performers or between a strong and an average performer (based on industry averages for return on equity and return on assets in the five years preceding the alliance) had a success rate of 67%, versus 39% for alliances involving two weaker players.

When one partner is weak, managing the alliance seems to be too great a distraction from improvements needed in other parts of the business. When unbalanced partnerships do succeed, it is usually because the strong partner brings the capability that is crucial to the venture; it pulls the weaker partner along for a while before acquiring it or finding another partner.

One U.S. pharmaceutical company underestimated the importance of having a strong joint venture partner when it paired with a relatively weak Japanese player. The U.S. company had a large share in its domestic market, a good portfolio of drugs, and strong R&D capabilities. Seeking to expand its position in Japan, it partnered with a second-tier company with a large sales force rather than one of the leading Japanese pharmaceutical companies, which might have had products that competed more directly.

The joint venture failed for several reasons. First, the sales force of the Japanese company was poorly managed and was unable to meet its targets for distributing the drugs of the Western partner. Second, over time, the Japanese partner was simply unable to push drugs that had been successful in other markets through Japan's development and approval process. It did not have insider contacts to guide the approval process, and it lacked the management resources and the capital to invest in commercialization. Even the excellent products and top-tier position of the Western partner could not compensate for its partner's shortcomings.

Most alliances formed chiefly to build the skills of a weaker partner meet with failure or mixed results. Only when the alliance has a solid business rationale other than self-improvement and a viable combined business system that draws on strengths from each partner can skills be transferred successfully.

Consider a joint venture between a weak European auto company seeking to improve its manufacturing effectiveness and a strong Japanese auto manufacturer.

The Japanese manufacturer, which wanted to produce a new compact car for the European market, was to provide design, body parts, and manufacturing technology—areas in which it excelled. The European partner was to provide capacity in an existing auto plant and local management. The European company was, however, financially strained and distracted by problems in its other car lines, and management was unable to give the new venture the time and energy it required. The venture ultimately failed, selling only 20% as many cars as projected.

Although skills transfer should not be the primary purpose of a joint venture, it often occurs naturally, and if the partners both bring specific strengths, both will benefit. In the GM-Suzuki joint venture in Canada, for example, both parents have contributed and gained. The alliance, CAMI Automotive, Inc., was formed to manufacture low-end cars for the U.S. market. The plant, run by Suzuki management, produces the Geo Metro/Suzuki Swift, the smallest, highest gas-mileage GM car sold in North America, as well as the Geo Tracker/Suzuki Sidekick sport utility vehicle. Through CAMI, Suzuki has gained access to GM's dealer network and an expanded market for parts and components. GM avoided the cost of developing low-end cars and obtained models it needed to help revitalize the lower end of the Chevrolet product line and to improve GM's average fuel economy rating. And the CAMI factory, which promises to be one of the most productive plants in North America once it reaches full capacity, has been a test bed for GM to learn how Japanese carmakers use work teams, run flexible assembly lines, and manage quality control.

While it is important that partners have complementary skills and capabilities, an even balance of strength is also crucial. This is especially true in product-for-market swaps. When one partner brings product or technology and the other brings access to desirable markets, there is often a certain amount of suspicion. Each partner fears that the other will try to usurp its proprietary advantage. Such fears are hardly unwarranted, since many prospective partners are competitors in some business arenas to begin with. A European chemical company formed a venture with a large Japanese company to produce and market its product to food manufacturers in Japan in the early 1980s. Within less than ten years, the Japanese partner had absorbed the production process technology and become its partner's biggest threat in the United States and Europe.

While it is effective for partners to bring complementary skills to the table—strong R&D paired with well-developed manufacturing processes, innovative products paired with solid and established distribution and sales capabilities—the strongest alliances exist when each partner brings both products and an established market presence in different geographic markets. The Toshiba-Motorola alliance is an example of getting the balance right: Toshiba brought expertise in DRAMs and access to Japan; Motorola brought expertise in microprocessors and access to the U.S. market. These alliances seem to have a more stable balance of power because neither partner relies solely on the other for technical expertise, products, or market entry. Fully 75% of the alliances serving at least two major markets—Europe, Japan, or the United States—succeeded. Only 43% succeeded when the venture focused on a single market—when, for example, one company traded products for its partner's access to customers.

Autonomy and Flexibility

The flexibility to evolve is a hallmark of successful alliances. Flexibility allows joint ventures to overcome problems and to adapt to changes over time. If they are to evolve, alliances also need the capacity to resolve conflicts. A partnership is best able to resolve or avoid conflicts when it has its own management team and a strong board with operational decision-making authority.

Flexibility is important because it is inevitable that the objectives, resources, and relative power of the parents will gradually change. Even the most astute parent companies cannot anticipate these trends and other events that will occur during the life of the alliance. Somewhere along the line, joint ventures are likely to find that their markets are shifting, new technologies are emerging, or customers' needs are changing. Also, the strategies, skills, and resources of the parents may change. And once alliances are up and running, they often discover new opportunities like a new market for their products or a new way to leverage their expertise.

Flexibility is also needed to overcome problems, which many alliances encounter in one form or another early on. Some 67% of the alliances in our sample ran into trouble in the first two years, and those that had the flexibility to evolve were better able to recover. Many joint ventures have trouble meeting their initial goals, often because the expectations or projections at the outset were overly optimistic. An R&D venture to develop a new plastics-recycling process was unable to meet cost targets because the partners had seriously underestimated the investments required to commercialize the new technology. And the president of an automotive joint venture reflected on his similar experience this way:

"If I were doing it over again, I'd insist on a more rigorous feasibility study. It is easy to be optimistic. Because of the reputation and experience of our parent companies, we figured we could get our automotive system specified in customers' cars rapidly. Not so. In the eyes of the customer, we were a new supplier of a safety-critical product and had to undergo seven or eight stringent engineering tests and validation steps with improvements and corrective action at each step. This took a minimum of two years with each customer. That's not to mention the fact that the investment levels were much higher than we expected."

The link between flexibility and success is strong. Nearly 40% of the alliances in our sample gradually broadened the scope of their initial charter. Some expanded into new geographic or product markets, others required major investments. Of those alliances that had evolved, 79% were successful and 89% are ongoing. In contrast, of the alliances whose scope remained unchanged, only 33% were successful and more than half have terminated.

The CFM International venture created by GE and Snecma in 1974 to collaborate on the development of jet engines is among those that evolved and flourished. The two companies initially focused on jointly developing and manufacturing the CFM56 engine, with 20,000 to 30,000 pounds of thrust. Subsequently, the two partners expanded their collaboration to spread the costs of developing a wider range of engines, including the larger CF6 series of engines. By 1991, the alliance had booked orders and commitments for more than 10,000 engines worth about $39 billion.

Similarly, GMF Robotics was set up in 1982 by GM and Fanuc to develop robotics for the auto industry. The venture has gradually broadened its focus and now sells robotics to nonautomotive customers in industries like food processing and computer manufacturing. And Toshiba and Motorola, building on an existing relationship, agreed in 1986 to create a joint venture to manufacture microprocessors and memory chips in Japan, and they continue to discuss other ways of expanding on their initial agreement.

Unlike the GM-Snecma, GM-Fanuc, and Toshiba-Motorola alliances, one joint venture between a U.S. and a foreign company to serve the minicomputer market in the United States did not deviate from its original plan and suffered because of it. The joint venture was conceived largely as a sales organization to sell to the U.S. market minicomputers designed and manufactured by the parent companies. The sales-oriented joint venture quickly fell behind in adapting products for the rapidly changing needs of banking customers in the United States. Friction quickly developed between the partners, and, ultimately, the venture floundered and was bought out. In hindsight, the joint venture might have recovered had its scope been expanded to include product development, manufacturing, and sales for a broader range of minicomputer products the parents offered.

Negotiating every aspect of the alliance in excruciating detail and spelling out the rules in legal documents will not guarantee healthy evolution. But there are ways to build in flexibility, namely by giving the alliance a strong president, a full business system of its own (R&D, manufacturing, marketing, sales, and distribution), complete decision-making power on operating issues, a powerful board, and a sense of identity. As the president of a successful U.S.-based joint venture put it, "The best way for parents to make a joint venture work is to give it the resources it needs, put someone they trust in charge, and leave him or her alone to do the job."

Parent companies typically retain responsibility for decisions about equity financing and overall governance structure, but operating decisions are best made by managers whose sole focus is the joint venture. This kind of hands-off approach requires that the parent companies structure and perceive the alliance as an entity in and of itself and not as part of either ongoing business. Ensuring that the alliance does not need to depend on either parent for basic operating functions reinforces the separateness and also simplifies coordination of those activities.

Giving the alliance strong leadership further encourages autonomy. Managers of successful alliances embrace their authority and build employee loyalty to the joint venture rather than to the parent companies. Such loyalty is not always easy to cultivate in light of the fact that key employees usually are drawn from the parent companies and are likely to return there. But strong leaders can win the support they need to operate as a freestanding business. Early on in the Toshiba-Motorola alliance, for example, engineers were reluctant to share semiconductor production technology with people who just months before had been their competitors. When senior management realized what was going on, it met with mid-level managers to convince them that the relationship was good for both parent companies overall, even though each specific area might not be benefiting.

Establishing a high-powered board is important. Sometimes alliances slip from top management's attention, which may be understandable since they are not really part of the parent companies' everyday operations.

In other cases, lack of a strong board for the venture creates delays as key decisions are passed up and down the parent organizations' chains of command. There are some exceptions to the rule about managerial autonomy. When joint ventures are formed to share R&D costs, for instance, R&D parents often need to stay closely involved to ensure that the R&D program fits with their customer needs and manufacturing capabilities. And when alliances are formed to coordinate activities performed by the partners at different stages in the value chain, the coordination may best be done directly between the parents without creating a separate joint venture organization. In these cases, a different rule applies: the responsibilities of each party must be clearly defined.

In the fifty-fifty venture between Petroleos de Venezuela (PDVSA) and Veba Oil, for example, PDVSA provided 50% of the crude oil supply, while Veba provided the other 50% and took clear responsibility for downstream refining and marketing. In Boeing's partnership with Fuji, Mitsubishi, Kawasaki, and Aeritalia to produce the Boeing 767, a separate joint venture entity was not created, and Boeing held overall control for coordination and management. These alliances would not be viable businesses without critical functions of the parents.

Fifty-Fifty Ownership

In structuring alliances, the issue of financial ownership should be separated from managerial control. In contrast to the conventional wisdom that fifty-fifty ownership spells failure because of stalled decision making, alliances with an even split of financial ownership are actually more likely to succeed than those in which one partner holds a majority interest (see the exhibit "Fifty-Fifty Alliances Are More Likely to Succeed"). When one parent has a majority stake, it tends to dominate decision making and put its own interests above those of its partner, or for that matter, of the joint venture itself. Both partners tend to be worse off as a consequence.

The autonomy and flexibility most alliances need are easiest to achieve when neither parent's investment outweighs the other's. Our evidence shows that joint ventures with an even split of ownership have a higher success rate (60%) than those in which one partner holds a majority stake (31%). For one thing, when ownership is

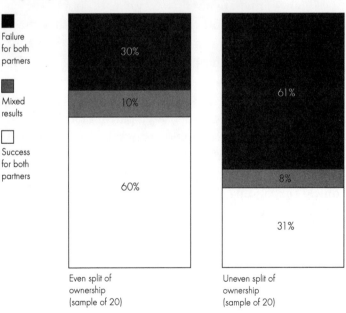

Fifty-Fifty Alliances Are More Likely to Succeed

Failure for both partners

Mixed results

Success for both partners

30%
10%
60%

61%
8%
31%

Even split of ownership (sample of 20)

Uneven split of ownership (sample of 20)

(Joint ventures only; excludes parent-to-parent equity stakes and nonequity alliances.)

even, it is more likely that the joint venture will be set up as a separate entity with its own strong management. But fifty-fifty ownership is important for another reason: it builds trust by ensuring that each partner is concerned about the other's success, or in the words of Stephen Levy, former head of Japan operations and a board member at Motorola, "Each partner has a stake in *mutual success.*"

When ownership is uneven, one parent typically exercises control, sometimes in ways that are not in the minority partner's interests. One majority partner shifted excess employees to the venture. When the bloated payroll contributed to cash flow problems, the partners had a showdown. Eventually, the minority partner gained more say in operating decisions, but only after threatening to withdraw from the venture.

Alliances that are not fifty-fifty can, of course, succeed. One way to boost the odds of success is to realize that the alliance is a win-win situation rather than a zero-sum game. In the 49 alliances we analyzed closely, only 3 resulted in success for one partner and failure for the other. In "unfair" alliances, both partners typically fail since the poorly compensated partner has little incentive to follow through on commitments. Indeed, it is particularly important to protect the interests of a minority partner. This is exactly the philosophy of the quickly expanding TRW-Koyo Steering Systems joint venture, which was established to serve Japanese transplant auto makers in the United States. Although TRW owned 51%, Arvind Korde, president of TRW-Koyo Steering Systems, treated it as if it were a fifty-fifty partnership. In Korde's words, the earmark of the venture's success was that, "At times, both TRW and Koyo thought I was too sensitive to the other partner."

Termination by Acquisition

Most alliances terminate, even successful ones. We found that, of the ventures that terminated, more than 75% were acquired by one of the partners. Yet companies don't always prepare for the eventual ending of their alliances, and some are caught off guard when the other partner is in a better position to buy it. If the seller didn't anticipate such an outcome, the acquisition can compromise its long-term strategic interests. Says the CEO of a global communications company, "One of the most important elements of global strategy is the balance between intermediate term and long-term initiatives. Joint ventures may fill intermediate-term needs but may also mortgage the long-term global future."

Alliances often terminate after meeting the partners' goals. Two Western-Japanese alliances—Sandoz-Sankyo and Bayer-Takeda—demonstrate the point that termination is not equivalent to failure. Both Sandoz and Bayer left their ventures after having achieved their goal of establishing independent businesses in Japan; both are ranked among the top 25 players in the Japanese pharmaceutical industry. Their Japanese partners, both of which are among the largest Japanese players, also benefited by gaining access to strong-selling drugs their Western partners had developed.

By 1990, when Sandoz and Sankyo agreed to dissolve their alliance, Sankyo was selling 22 Sandoz drugs, which took in ¥82 billion in revenues. Sandoz and Sankyo are continuing to cooperate with each other and are planning a phased withdrawal over four years of five key Sandoz drugs from Sankyo's sales channels. Sankyo is also helping Sandoz build its marketing force by sending personnel to Sandoz's Japan operations.

Similarly, Bayer, which owns 75.6% of Bayer Yakuhin, a joint venture in which Takeda owns 14.6% and Yoshitomi Pharmaceuticals owns 9.8%, recently dissolved its 80-year sales agreement with Takeda in order to sell Bayer-brand pharmaceuticals through its own channels. Takeda had previously sold an estimated ¥60 billion worth of Bayer drugs annually on a consignment basis.

Some joint ventures end less amicably and fairly. Shifts in the parents' geographic position, functional strengths, and technological position can make one parent emerge as the "natural buyer" (see the exhibit "Alliances Are Usually Acquired by a Major Partner"). By the time that happens, it may be too late for the seller to protect its interests. Take, for instance, the alliance between two specialty chemical companies. One was to provide product formulas and manufacturing know-how; the other was to provide marketing and distribution to its existing industrial customers. Over a ten-year period, though, the "sales" partner was able to improve on the basic process technology to tailor products to its customers. Then in a clear position of strength, since its people had the customer relationships and knew the technology, it offered to buy out the business. The "technology" partner, faced with the threat that its partner would go it alone anyway if it refused to sell, divested its share. The seller made a handsome profit but ended up with zero position in a major market and little chance of reentering in the future.

Often the natural buyer is the company that is most willing to invest to build the joint venture. Here companies that have deep pockets and look to strategic results, not financial returns, as the measure of success are at an advantage. It is important that alliance negotiators understand the differing goals and perspectives of poten-

Alliances Are Usually Acquired by a Major Partner

Partnership	Start Date	Acquired By	Acquisition Date
Asahi-Dow	1952	Asahi	1982
Merck-Banyu	1954	Merck	1983
Crédit Suisse-First Boston	1978	Crédit Suisse	1988
Toshiba-Rank	1978	Toshiba	1980
Fujitsu-TRW	1980	Fujitsu	1983
Du Pont-Philips (PD Magnetics)	1981	Philips	1988
Fiat-Rockwell	1981	Rockwell	1987
Mitsubishi-Verbatim	1982	Mitsubishi	1990
VW-Seat	1982	VW	1990
Sony-CBS (Digital Audio Disc Corporation)	1983	Sony	1985
Siemens-Telecom Plus International	1984	Siemens	1987
NatWest-Banca March	1985	NatWest	1989
Nestlé-Rothmans	1986	Nestlé	1988
Fujitsu-GTE	1987	Fujitsu	1988

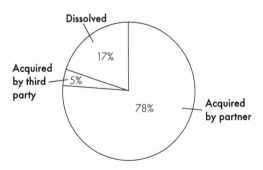

(Sample of 18 terminated partnerships.)

tial partners as they form cross-border ventures. Western managers in particular often fail to balance the attractiveness of Japanese capital with the possibility that Japanese partners may become buyers of the business. Japanese companies are often able to pay more for their acquisitions because they have a lower cost of capital and longer time horizons for investments. But our research suggests that Japanese companies do not earn back even their *own* relatively low cost of capital in two-thirds of cross-border acquisition programs. And a survey of 90 mid-level managers at 25 leading Japanese companies found that 85% of the respondents thought that entering new businesses or improving the position of existing ones is more important than financial gain. This is in sharp contrast to the profit orientation of many Western executives.

These factors suggest that Japanese partners are often well positioned to buy the joint venture. Indeed, a separate study by the McKinsey & Company Tokyo office including more than 700 alliances between Japanese and non-Japanese companies indicated that Japanese partners have been the acquirers in approximately 70% of the terminating alliances.

One steel joint venture between U.S. and Japanese partners is typical. Over time, the U.S. investors have been unwilling to sink additional capital into modernizing factories, but the Japanese have been, and their stake has grown with each additional investment. As the business continues to require additional capital, the U.S. partner is likely to be reduced to a distinct minority.

The tendency of Japanese companies to be buyers of their ventures can be good news for Western partners that want to improve position or develop products before divesting a business. But it may make for a troubled relationship: if the Western company is looking for an early return, it is likely to seek the largest, hence most threatening, Japanese players as partners and rely on them to manage the venture. The venture may be profitable, but the Western partner's contribution to the business may shrink over time, and the Japanese company might eventually buy its partner out.

If, however, the non-Japanese partner continues to contribute in a significant way, the joint venture can grow and change. One example of a successful and enduring U.S.-Japanese alliance is Fujitsu-Amdahl. Fujitsu initially brought capital and manufacturing skills to the party, while Amdahl brought expertise in mainframe design and architecture, as well as an established local name in the United States. Since 1972, Fujitsu has increased its equity stake in Amdahl to about 44% but has agreed not to increase its ownership beyond 49.5% through April 1994. With Fujitsu's help as a financial backer and component supplier, Amdahl has been able to meet the rising ante to develop new mainframe machines, and its rank among U.S. computer companies has risen from nineteenth in 1980 to thirteenth in 1990.

Companies can retain the option to buy the venture by holding a 50% or greater stake. In addition, they should be actively involved in the ongoing operation of the joint venture. And they should be sure to place people in positions where they can learn the critical skills the venture needs to operate independently. There are reasons, though, to choose to be the seller. If, for instance, a company is exiting a business, a joint venture allows the eventual buyer to learn the business before taking it over.

Intellectual property rights and proprietary technologies are ticklish areas in an ongoing alliance, but they become even more sensitive when the partners separate. Legal protections go only so far. Successful alliance partners tend to use several different structural tactics to meet this challenge. First, they isolate sensitive technologies from the venture. For example, GE modularized the production of high value-added engine-core components to protect its know-how from Snecma. Similarly, Boeing retained control of overall design and assembly of key components in its alliances with Mitsubishi, Fuji, Kawasaki, and Aeritalia.

Second, some companies centralize contact points between the joint venture and the parents. This is relatively easy in highly centralized companies—like Japanese businesses—but poses a challenge in more open and decentralized organizations, like many in the West. Third, fixed costs that are so high they must be shared and complementary staff make it hard for either partner to succeed without the other. Both Toshiba's and Motorola's strategic position would be damaged if either terminated the alliance because the two companies have such a high level of interdependence in the form of shared factories, shared distribution, and complementary specialized skills.

Strategic alliances are tough to pull off, but they are often necessary. Greenfield strategies take a long time, acquisition targets aren't always available, and simpler approaches like licensing may not be responsive enough. While every alliance is unique, there is a lot to be learned from the lessons of existing partnerships.

But managers need to remember that alliances by their nature are laden with tensions. No matter how well structured they are, most alliances get into trouble at one point or another. Strong companies make attractive partners, but they also present a competitive threat over time. The objectives and styles of parents will differ. Neither fifty-fifty nor majority ownership is a guarantee of fair or good management decisions. And as the venture grows, tensions will arise between the parents and between each parent and the venture.

These inherent tensions require more flexibility on the part of the parents than many other business strategies. Alliance managers should not only structure the alliance to minimize these tensions but also be prepared to rebalance the alliance—or exit smoothly—when it gets into trouble. Meeting the requirements of change, after all, is the main requirement for success in alliances.

How We Defined Success

TO BE CONSIDERED SUCCESSFUL, an alliance had to pass two tests: both partners achieved their ingoing strategic objectives and both recovered their financial costs of capital. Progress on the strategic objectives was based on market share, sales volume, new product development, or other criteria specific to the alliance. Our evaluation of financial and strategic success relied heavily on access to unpublished financial results and on interviews with company insiders and industry experts, as well as public information.

For acquisition programs exceeding 20% of the acquirer's market value, we assessed whether the acquirer was able to maintain or improve its return on equity and return on assets. For smaller acquisition programs, we conducted interviews and assessed financial results to determine whether the return equaled or exceeded the companies' cost of capital.

We should note that these financial criteria for success are distinctly American. Most Japanese and many European companies have longer term, less financially oriented means for judging their purchases.

Manager's Choice: Expand Abroad or Diversity at Home?

EXPANDING AT HOME IN CORE businesses is often the most appealing growth strategy. But in many mature industries, it is not an option. Managers are left with the choice of diversifying at home or expanding abroad. On the one hand, most CEOs remember the "sins of the seventies"—the rash of acquisitions conglomerates made in a wide range of unrelated businesses, which left a legacy of poor business performance. On the other hand, given the added challenges of managing across borders, many managers are reluctant to make cross-border acquisitions or alliances.

In fact, we found that expanding through cross border alliances or acquisitions is often a much more attractive option than diversifying by acquiring domestically. Cross-border alliances and acquisitions have a success rate of somewhat better than 50%, compared with the success rate of about 25% for home-country diversification programs.*

Why? In cross-border alliances, partners can avoid acquisition premiums while combining their strengths to target core or related businesses. And most cross-border acquirers focus their sights on core businesses, where there is more opportunity to add value than in related businesses.

*Data on domestic mergers and acquisitions are from a 1986 McKinsey study of 200 top companies.

Originally published in November–December 1991
Reprint 91602

About the Contributors

JOEL BLEEKE is coauthor with David Ernst of "Is Your Strategic Alliance Really a Sale?" and "The Way to Win in Cross-Border Alliances." He was a Director in McKinsey & Company's Chicago office, as well as a leader of the Firm's financial institutions practice and its strategic alliances practice. He wrote extensively on deregulation, alliances, and other issues. He served numerous *Fortune* 500 companies on top management issues. He passed away at age forty-four after battling cancer in a way that was inspiring to his colleagues and friends.

HENRY W. CHESBROUGH is the Class of 1961 Fellow and Assistant Professor at the Harvard Business School. The author of three *Harvard Business Review* articles to date, his research focuses on new models for organizing technology and innovation, and blends academic research with management experience. Prior to becoming an academic, he worked for ten years in Silicon Valley in marketing and product management roles. His book *Open Innovation: The New Imperative for Creating and Profiting from Technology* will be published in early 2003 by Harvard Business School Publishing.

YVES L. DOZ is the Dean of Executive Education and the Timken Chaired Professor of Global Technology and Innovation at INSEAD. His research on the strategy of multinational companies, examining specifically high-technology industries, led to numerous publications, including three books: *Government Control and Multinational Management, Strategic Management in Multinational Companies,* and (with C.K. Prahalad) *The Multinational Mission: Balancing Local Demands and Global Vision.* Professor Doz currently carries out research on strategic partnerships and technological cooperation between companies, on global competition in the knowledge economy, and on the competitive revitalization of international companies.

DAVID ERNST is coauthor with Joel Bleeke of "Is Your Strategic Alliance Really a Sale?" and "The Way to Win in Cross-Border Alliances." He is a Principal in McKinsey's Washington, D.C., office. He leads the Firm's strategic alliances practice, and has served numerous global companies on strategy, growth, and alliance issues. His perspectives on alliances and acquisitions have been published in more than forty articles.

CARLOS GHOSN is president of Nissan Motor Corp., Ltd. Mr. Ghosn is also a member of the board of directors. He joined Nissan on June 25, 1999. Prior to joining Nissan, Mr. Ghosn joined Renault in October 1996 and was appointed executive vice president in charge of general management in December 1996. As executive vice president of Renault, his responsibilities included advanced research, vehicle engineering and development, powertrain operations, purchasing, manufacturing, and the MERCOSUR business unit in Latin America. Mr. Ghosn was born in Brazil and holds engineering degrees from the Ecole Polytechnique and the Ecole des Mines de Paris. Mr. Ghosn is married and has three daughters and one son.

BENJAMIN GOMES-CASSERES is now a professor at Brandeis University and was previously at Harvard Business

School. His book *The Alliance Revolution: The New Shape of Business Rivalry* elaborates on his ideas in this volume. He is coauthor of *Mastering Alliance Strategy: A Comprehensive Guide to Design, Management, and Organization* and has been a consultant to companies worldwide. His work is online at AllianceStrategy.com, which gives additional resources for managers.

GARY HAMEL is Visiting Professor of Strategic and International Management at the London Business School and Chairman of Strategos, an international consulting company. He has published numerous articles in the *Harvard Business Review, Fortune, Sloan Management Review*, and the *Wall Street Journal* and has introduced such breakthrough concepts as strategic intent, core competence, corporate imagination, expeditionary marketing, and strategy as stretch. His book with C.K. Prahalad, *Competing for the Future*, has been hailed by many journals as one of the decade's most influential business books, and by *BusinessWeek* as "Best Management Book of the Year."

ROSABETH MOSS KANTER is the Ernest L. Arbuckle Professor of Business Administration at Harvard Business School, specializing in strategy, innovation, and leadership for change. She advises major corporations and governments worldwide, and is the author or coauthor of fifteen books, including her latest book, *Evolve!: Succeeding in the Digital Culture of Tomorrow*. In 2001 she received the Academy of Management's Distinguished Career Award, its highest award for scholarly contributions, for her impact on management thought. She cofounded Goodmeasure Inc., a consulting group, and serves as chairman of its board as well as serving as a director or adviser for other companies.

ASHISH NANDA is Associate Professor in the Negotiations, Organizations, and Markets unit at the Harvard Business

School. His research focuses on management of professional service organizations. Nanda has advised and taught on the subjects of management of professional service firms, business ethics, and international management. His professional activities have included projects with law, investment and commercial banking, management consulting, accounting, IT consulting, executive search, advertising, and international commercial firms in North America, United Kingdom, India, France, Switzerland, and Latin America. Prior to coming to Harvard University, he worked as an executive with the Tata group of companies in India. Nanda received a Bachelor of Technology degree (First Rank) in Electrical Engineering from the Indian Institute of Technology at Delhi and Post Graduate Diploma in Management (First Rank) from the Indian Institute of Management at Ahmedabad. He was awarded an A.M. in Economics from Harvard University in 1990, and a Ph.D. in Business Economics from Harvard Business School in 1993.

C.K. PRAHALAD, D.B.A., has been named a 2001 top-10 worldwide management thinker by the *Financial Times*, the *Observer*, and *Business Week*. He has coauthored several *Harvard Business Review* articles, including "Core Competence of the Corporation," with Gary Hamel, and also coauthored *Competing for the Future* with Gary Hamel. He is a Harvey C. Fruehauf Professor of Business Administration at the University of Michigan Graduate School of Business Administration, Ann Arbor. Dr. Prahalad specializes in corporate strategy and the role and value of top management in large, diversified, multinational corporations. Dr. Prahalad has consulted with the top management of AT&T, Cargill, Eastman Kodak, Honeywell, ICL, Philips, TRW, Quantum, NCR, and Oracle.

DAVID J. TEECE is the Mitsubishi Bank Professor at the Haas School of Business, University of California, Berkeley. He has published over 150 books and articles, many of them on technological innovation and business organization. Notable contributions include "Profiting from Technological Innovation," *Research Policy* (which is the most cited article in the journal's history), and *Managing Intellectual Capital* (Oxford University Press, 2000). Professor Teece is also Executive Chairman of LECG, an expert services firm with over 600 employees worldwide.

PETER J. WILLIAMSON is Professor of International Management and Asian Business at the INSEAD in Fontainebleau, France, and Singapore. His research and publications span globalization, strategy innovation, and alliances. His latest book, *From Global to Metanational: How Companies Win in the Global Knowledge Economy* (HBS Press), sets out a blueprint for how multinationals can prosper in the global knowledge economy by developing their capability for "learning from the world." His other books include: *Managing the Global Frontier*, *The Economics of Financial Markets*, and *The Strategy Handbook*. Formerly at The Boston Consulting Group, he acts as consultant to companies in Europe, Asia, and the Americas and serves on the boards of several listed companies. He holds a Ph.D. in Business Economics from Harvard University.

Index